THE
ENGLISH
GARDENS
ALMANAC

Published in association with the English Tourist Board

Bloomsbury Books · London

First published by Lochar Publishing Ltd.
Moffat, Scotland DG10 9ED.

This edition published by Bloomsbury Books, an imprint of
The Godfrey Cave Group, 42 Bloomsbury Street, London, WC1B 3QJ,
under licence from Eric Dobby Publishing Ltd,
12 Warnford Road, Orpington, Kent BR6 6LW, 1993

Printed and bound in Great Britain by
BPCC Hazell Books Ltd

Member of BPCC Ltd

ISBN 1 85471 124 5

INTRODUCTION

The passion that the English as a nation have for gardening has produced some of the finest gardens in the world, spanning centuries in age and style and highlighting many aspects of England's past. Gardens can be all things to all people. They can offer peace and beauty, fresh air and exercise, a chance for the amateur gardener to learn from the expert, and for the family to enjoy an entertaining, relaxing day out together.

This guide contains a selection of some of the best known gardens open to the public with reasonable frequency across the country. The gardens featured range from seventeenth-century, formally laid-out gardens, through eighteenth-century landscaped gardens to the terraces and magnificent flower-beds of nineteenth-century gardens.

Individual entries are illustrated in colour and provide all the practical information you need to plan and enjoy your visit. A concise description mentions the garden's history and any special features. Up-to-date information is given on location, opening times, admission charges, facilities and accessibility for disabled visitors.

Every effort has been made to ensure that the information given is correct; however, details can change. Please check before setting out, especially if you have any special requirements.

GLOSSARY

ALLEY   A narrow walk, cut through dense woodland or formed by planting trees, trimmed on each side to give a wall-like effect.

ARBOUR   A bower or retreat, either made of trained trees or climbing plants grown on a framework; or an ornamental structure of metal or stone with a dome.

AVENUE   A road or walk planted with trees on either side.

BEEBOLE   A niche in a wall, usually at ground level and arched at the top, in which straw bee-skeps were placed in the winter up until the nineteenth century.

BELVEDERE   A place from which a 'fair view' may be observed. Usually a roof-top or tower-top turret, but can also be a tower built in a position commanding a fine view.

BOSKET   A thicket or plantation of trees forming part of the design of a park or garden.

CLAIR-VOYEE   Literally, a 'clear view': an opening in a wall or hedge, sometimes protected by a grille or screen, which allows a garden vista to continue into the countryside beyond.

CRINKLE-CRANKLE   A wall built in serpentine fashion. The bays often supply shelter for fruit trees.

EYE-CATCHER   Any feature in a landscape garden which creates a visual focal point.

FOLLY   A usually bizarre structure, built to surprise but having no practical function. Follies include: grottos, mock ruins, pyramids and stone circles.

GAZEBO   A place from which to gaze about. Usually a turret or garden house commanding a view.

GROTTO   A small cave, which may be natural or artificial.

HA-HA   A boundary between garden and park in the form of a deep, wide ditch, creating a barrier against farm animals without interupting the view.

KNOT   A bed laid out in an intricate pattern made from low-clipped or naturally low-growing plants. They were designed to be viewed from raised terraces or upstairs windows.

MAZE   A puzzle layout of paths, with dead ends, many alternative and confusing turnings, usually enclosed in hedges.

MOUNT   An artificial hill within a garden, built against an outer wall or free standing, to allow views across the surrounding countryside.

ORANGERY   A precursor of the greenhouse, they are typically tall buildings with long, narrow windows in stone walls. Some later examples have glass lights in the roof.

PARTERRE   A level garden area containing a number of flower-beds, separated from the rest of the garden in a formal way. Beds often laid out as *knots*.

PATTED'OIE   Literally, 'goose's foot'. A number of alleys or vistas radiating in a fan pattern from a central point.

PERGOLA   A structure of uprights and horizontal beams enclosing a walk below and acting as a support for climbing plants.

POTAGER   An ornamental kitchen garden planted with vegetables, fruit and herbs in edged beds.

TOPIARY   The art of clipping or training evergreen trees and bushes into shapes.

VISTA   A relatively confined view usually channelled by trees on either side, or along a valley.

VISTA-CLOSER   A building, obelisk or urn placed at the end of a vista as a focal end-point.

ANGLESEY ABBEY

Lode, Cambridgeshire, CB5 9EJ.
(0223) 81200

Ownership: National Trust.

Status: National Trust.

General Description: The Gardens and Abbey as they stand today were created through the vision of one man, Huttleston Broughton. The hyacinth garden and wonderful shows of daffodils and narcissi in spring, herbaceous borders and dahlia beds in summer, fine lawns and exotic tree species, together combine to offer something for every season. Over the years Lord Fairhaven built up a magnificent collection of statuary from simple shepherds to mythical beasts, lions to Roman emperors and Greek gods. In the north of the garden is the Lode mill, still working and the site of a mill since the Domesday Book.

Open: 28th March to 12th July: Wednesday to Sunday and Bank Holidays, 11 a.m. – 5.30 p.m. 13th July to 8th September daily 11a.m. – 5.30 p.m. 9th September to 18th October: Wednesday to Sunday, 11 a.m. – 5.30 p.m.

Admission: Wednesday to Saturday: £2.25; Sunday and Bank Holiday: £2.50 (Gardens only). Wednesdays and Saturdays: £4.50; Sunday and Bank Holidays: £5.50.

Facilities: Visitors' centre, restaurant, National Trust shop, free parking.

Disabled Access: Easy to Gardens, very limited to Abbey.

Additional Information: Picnic area with tables.

ANTONY

Torpoint, Cornwall PL11 2QA.
(0752) 812191

Status: National Trust.

General Description: Early eighteenth-century house in superb setting above Tamar Estuary. Landscape setting shows influence of Humphry Repton who produced one of his first Red Books for this site. Lawns sweep down to the Tamar and are edged to the west with clipped yew hedges. Topiary includes tall wigwam shape. Wall of old kitchen garden bordered by espaliered fruit trees and row of magnolias, Sheltered flower garden beyond yew hedge provides colourful summer display and terraces are planted with roses. NCCPG National collection of day lilies is based here. Garden also features a knot garden planted with box and germander. Grounds include fine specimen trees such as ginkgo and cork oak.

Open: 1st April to 29th October: Tuesday, Wednesday, Thursday and Bank Holiday Mondays plus Sundays in June, July and August, 1.30 p.m. – 5.30 p.m. Last admission half hour before closing.

Admission: £3.20. Pre-booked parties: £2.40.

Facilities: Shop, toilets.

Disabled Access: Garden largely accessible to wheelchair users.

ARLEY HALL AND GARDENS

Near Northwich, Cheshire, CW9 6NA.
(0565) 777353. Fax: (0565) 777465

Ownership: The Hon. Michael and Mrs. Flower.

Status: Privately owned estate.

General Description: The gardens at Arley overlook beautiful parkland and provide a great variety of style and design. They extend to over twelve acres and rank among the finest in the country. Their main framework was laid out in the nineteenth century and perhaps the most outstanding creation is the double herbaceous border, one of the earliest to be established in England (1846). Other features dating from that period include the fine yew hedges and the Furlong Walk, an avenue of pleached lime trees and the Ilex Avenue. During the last twenty-five years major innovations have been carried out. A kitchen garden enclosure has been converted to a walled garden, there is an interesting collection of hybrid and specie roses. Features include the rockery, a scented garden, a herb garden and a vinery. Winner of the Christies/HHA Garden of the Year Award in 1987.

Open: 29th March to 4th October: Tuesdays to Sundays plus Bank Holidays, 12 noon – 5 p.m. Last admission to gardens 4.30 p.m., last admission to Hall 4 p.m.

Admission: Grounds, Gardens, Chapel – Adult: £2.50; Child under 17: £1.25; Children under 8 (when with a family visit only): free. Hall – Adult: £1.50 extra; Child under 17: 75p extra; Children under 8 free. Special prices for group visits.

Facilities: Ample free parking, lunches and light refreshments in Tudor Barn, gift shop, plants from Arley Gardens for sale.

Disabled Access: Yes.

Additional Information: Picnic area, dogs allowed on a leash.

BARRINGTON COURT GARDEN

Barrington, Ilminster, Somerset, TA19 0NQ.
(0985) 847777 – Ivan Smith, National Trust Regional Office for Information

Ownership: The National Trust.

Status: The National Trust.

General Description: Barrington Court Garden includes the Kitchen Garden where apple, pear and plum trees are trained along high stone walls. Walk through the formal walled garden laid out in a series of three rooms, the White garden, the Iris Garden and the Lily Garden influenced by Gertrude Jekyll.

Open: 7th April to 7th November: daily except Friday and Saturday, 12 a.m. – 5.30 p.m. Last admission 5 p.m. Courthouse open Wednesdays only 1.30 p.m. – 5 p.m., 1st April to 1st November guided tours only, 50p.

Admission: Adult: £3.00; Child: £1.50; Party: £2.50 (child: £1.20).

Facilities: Plant and garden sales, restaurant in the former beagle kennels serving hot and cold lunches and afternoon teas.

Disabled Access: Yes.

Additional Information: No dogs.

BATSFORD ARBORETUM

Moreton-in-Marsh, Glos., GL56 9QF.
(0608) 50722, (0386) 700409 weekends

Ownership: The Batsford Foundation.

Status: Historic Houses Association.

General Description: The Arboretum was established in the 1880's by Lord Redesdale as a 'wild garden', on his return from Japan, where he had been attached to the British Embassy. Strong influences from the Orient evident in the trees, bamboo and bronzes. It is one of the largest privately-owned collections of trees in the British Isles. Its fifty acres contain many rarities and offer superb views across the Vale of Evenlode. The springtime carpets of naturalised bulbs are followed by many magnolias, flowering cherries and the spectacular 'handerkerchief' tree. Later the large collection of maples and many varieties of sorbus provide wonderful autumn colour.

Open: Daily, 1st March to early November, 10 a.m. – 5 p.m.

Admission: Adults: £2; Senior Citizens, Children under 16: £1.50.

Facilities: Parking, garden centre, refreshments (licensed).

Disabled Access: Terrain unsuitable for wheelchair users.

Additional Information: Picnic area adjacent to car park, dogs permitted on leads.

BEDGEBURY NATIONAL PINETUM

Gouldhurst, Cranbrook, Kent, TN17 2SL.
(0580) 211044.

Ownership: Forestry Commission.

General Description: Established as the national collection of conifers in 1925. Plants were collected in the wild and raised by Kew and the collection is now reputed to be the most comprehensive in Europe and the best of its type in the World. Bedgebury Pinetum is established and landscaped around a lake and two main streams, and rhododendrons, azalean maples and other less common broadleaved species enhance the collection. It is a fascinating place for the tree specialist, and a beautiful place for the general visitor. The peace and quiet here give everyone an uplifting experience, young and not so young like.

Open: Every day 10 a.m. – 8 p.m. or dusk (whichever is earlier). Visitor Centre: 11 a.m. – 5 p.m., daily, Easter to September, weekends only October.

Admission: Adult: £1.50; Senior Citizen: £1; Child: 75p. Season: 12 months – Adult: £10; Child: £5; Family: £25.

Facilities: Free parking, toilets, information centre and florest shop, drinks and snacks also sold.

Disabled Access: Disabled car park and toilets.

Additional Information: Picnics welcome, except barbecues, dogs are allowed on leads only. A dog exercise area and dog free zone are also in operation.

BELSAY HALL, CASTLE AND GARDENS

Belsay, Newcastle Upon Tyne, NE20 0DX
(0661) 881636

Ownership: Sir Stephen Middleton, guardianship with
English Heritage.

Status: English Heritage.

General Description: Thirteenth-century towerhouse,
seventeenth-century manor house and nineteenth-century
neo-classical hall, thirty acres of magnificent parkland and
landscaped gardens including winter garden, terrace and
quarry garden. New wooded walk to be opened in Summer
season 1992. Spectacular rhododendron garden with species
that flowers from December, the winter gardens planted with
winter flowering heaths and heathers. The terrace garden with
magnolia trees and formal borders. The meadow garden is
full of wild flowers and surrounded by unusual trees.

Open: Summer, 1st April or Maundy Thursday to 30th
September, open every day 10 a.m. – 6 p.m. Winter: open
Tuesday – Sunday 10 a.m. – 4 p.m.

Admission: Adult: £2.10; Concession: £1.60; Children:
£1.10. 15% discount on parties of eleven or more.

Facilities: Exhibition, shop, A.V. with video about castles,
tea room open during Summer season.

Disabled Access: Access to ground floor of hall and gardens,
and a disabled toilet.

Additional Information: Dogs allowed on leads, picnic
tables in car park.

BICTON PARK GARDENS

East Budleigh, Budleigh Salterton, Devon, EX9 7DP.
(0395) 68889

Ownership: Bicton Park Trust Co.

Status: Private Charitable Trust.

General Description: Bicton Park is the carefully tended home of native and exotic plants from around the world, displayed in a variety of gardens and special settings. After a chequered history, the eighteenth century saw it pass to the progressive and benevolent Lord Henry Rolle, who laid down the Italian Gardens, from a design by Andre le Nôtre, creator of the famous gardens at Versailles. But it was not until nearly half a century later that it was crowned by the building of the pillared temple and Orangeries, and flanked by glasshouses which now exhibit some wonderful collections of orchids, geraniums and fuchsias. The years since have seen many additions, including the famous Palm House which houses a tropical collection of plants, the Pinetum with its unique collection of rare conifers and the American Garden filled with plants and shrubs from the Rolle family estates in Bermuda and Florida. More recently we have seen the introduction of the Bicton Woodland Railway, with its extension to the Hermitage in 1975, and the formation of one of the finest collections of agricultural and estate memorabilia in the country can be found in the James Countryside Museum. New concepts, such as the Oriental Gardens have been formed to create 'atmospheres' rather than formal displays. A Bird Garden and Tropical World have been added to the extensive Children's Fun World and Play-area to provide a wealth of interest and fun, whilst at no time is it forgotten that the Trust's main purpose is in the restoration of its fine buildings and statues, and the conservation for future generations of one of England's finest gardens.

Open: Daily, 10 a.m. – 6 p.m., April to September. Daily 10 a.m. – 4 p.m., March and October.

Admission: 'All Inclusive Admission' – Adult: £4.70; Child (3 – 15): £3.70; Senior Citizens: £3.95. 'Return Ticket' – Adult: £1.50; Child: £1.00.

Facilities: Restaurant, bar, free parking, reductions for groups of twenty or more.

Disabled Access: Disabled toilets, ramps, specially adapted carriage on woodland railway.

Additional Information: Gift shop, plant shop, picnic areas, dogs allowed on leads.

BLENHEIM PALACE

Woodstock, Oxfordshire, OX20 1PX.
(0993) 811091

Ownership: His Grace the Duke of Marlborough.

Status: Historic Houses Association, Treasure Houses of England.

General Description: Blenheim Palace is the home of the 11th Duke of Marlborough and the birthplace of Sir Winston Churchill, whose memory is celebrated by his birthroom and an Exhibition. Built for John Churchill, 1st Duke of Marlborough, from 1705 to 1722 in recognition of his victory at The Battle of Blenheim 1704. The Palace is set in over 2,000 acres of landscaped parkland ('Capability' Brown) and its architect was Sir John Vanbrugh. Formal gardens (Achille Duchêne) grace the east and west fronts, and to the south immaculate lawns sweep down to the pleasure grounds, arboretum and lake. Also, rose garden, sunken and walled gardens.

Open: Palace open daily from mid March to end October 10.30 a.m. (last entry 4.45 p.m.). Park open daily all year 9.00 a.m. – 5.30 p.m. (last entry 4.45 p.m.).

Admission: Adults: £6; Senior Citizens/Students: £4.50; Children: £3.00.

Facilities: Restaurant and two cafeterias, motor launch on lake, narrow gauge railway, four gift shops, garden centre, adventure playground. Optional extras: The Marlborough Maze and Rowing Boat hire.

Disabled Access: Entry to Palace via ramps – once inside all on one level. Disabled toilets in Palace and in Park.

Additional Information: Picnics, dogs on leads allowed in Park.

BLICKLING HALL

Blickling, Norwich, NR11 6NF.
(0263) 733084

Ownership: National Trust.

Status: National Trust.

General Description: Blickling Hall, a superb Jacobean mansion, was built for Sir Henry Hobart, Lord Chief Justice to James I. Whilst the exterior of this house has changed little during the 370 years since it was built the gardens have changed five times in the same period, following the dictates of fashion and fancy over the years. This has resulted in an extremely interesting combination of formal pastures and wilderness within the forty-three acres confined by the ha-ha with beautiful views over the park with its serpentine lake. Herbaceous borders best in July/August.

Open: 28th March to 1st November: Tuesday, Wednesday, Friday, Saturday and Sunday (closed Good Friday). Hall: 1 p.m. – 5 p.m. Garden 12 a.m. – 5 p.m. (Shop open 12. a.m. Restaurant open 11 a.m.)

Admission: House and Garden: £4.90. Garden only: £2.30. Park free.

Facilities: Car park, restaurant, shop, garden, plant centre.

Disabled Access: Ramps for wheelchairs, adapted toilets, lift in hall, separate car park near entrance.

Additional Information: Picnic area in old orchard, no dogs allowed in garden, allowed in park on a lead.

BORDE HILL GARDEN

Borde Hill Lane, Haywards Heath, West Sussex, RH16 1XP.
(0444) 450326

Ownership: Borde Hill Garden Limited.

Status: Privately owned.

General Description: Borde Hill Garden was bought by the
Stephenson Clarke family in 1892. Some plantings started
immediately whilst expeditions to China, Burma, Tibet, Chile
and Tasmania were supported during the following twenty or
so years to establish this now unique and outstanding
collection of plants. Individual specimens of oaks from
Southern France, North America, Caucasus and North Africa,
Cyprus etc. can be found in the South park; poplars and
maples from China and Japan in Lullings Ghyll. Both North
and South parks have specimens of firs, pines etc. although
the gales have severely depleted the Pinetum and other areas.
The woodland walk through Warren Wood and on into
Stephanies Glade is a pleasing mixture of trees, shrubs
(mainly rhododendrons) and wild flowers. Camellia Donation
was first raised here; there is a large collection of magnolias,
including Magnolia Delavayi in the Walled Garden which
was planted in 1911 and is the Chinese equivalent of
Magnolia Grandiflora. Recent developments include a lake
which has opened up the parkland to visitors and an
interesting Children's Playground constructed with trees
which fell in the 1987 gale.

Open: Daily, 28th March to 25th October, 10 a.m. – 6 p.m.

Admission: 28th March to 14th June – Adults: £3; Senior Citizens: £2; Children: £1. 15th June to 25th October – Adults: £2; Senior Citizens and groups of twenty or more: £1.25; Children: 75p.

Facilities: Free parking, licensed tearooms and restaurant, plant sales, small shop, conference centre.

Disabled Access: All facilities and majority of garden accessible to wheelchair users.

Additional Information: Picnic area by lake, children's playground, dogs allowed on lead.

BOWOOD HOUSE AND GARDENS

Calne, Wiltshire, SN11 0LZ.
(0249) 812102

Ownership: The Earl of Shelburne.

Status: Historic Houses Association.

General Description: Bowood House, ancestral home of the Earl and Countess of Shelburne, is surrounded by one of England's loveliest parks. Created by 'Capability' Brown in the 1760's, the gardens extend over ninety acres. The Rhododendron Walks, situated in a separate fifty acre park are open for six weeks during May and June. The entrance and car park are approximately two miles from the main Bowood entrance. The House is a wonderful example of Georgian architecture designed by Robert Adam. On the ground floor is a magnificent library which houses 5,000 volumes, a laboratory in which Dr. Joseph Priestly discovered oxygen gas in 1774 and the Orangery which was converted into a picture gallery by the present Earl's father.

Open: House and Gardens – 1st April to 1st November: open every day from 11 a.m. – 6 p.m. Rhododendron Walks – open six weeks during May and June: daily 11 a.m. – 6 p.m.

Admission: Adults: £4.30; Senior Citizens: £3.50; Children: £2.10.

Facilities: Large car park, garden tearoom, licensed restaurant, sandwich box, ice cream kiosk, plant centre and gift shop.

Disabled Access: Disabled toilets on arrival and in the house. Disabled parking by arrangement, upper floors of house inaccessible.

Additional Information: Picnic area at far end of the car park, picnics allowed in the grounds.

BRAMHAM PARK

Bramham Park, Wetherby, West Yorkshire.
(0937) 844265

Ownership: Mr. George Lane Fox.

Status: Historic Houses Association.

General Description: Bramham Park is a splendid Queen
Anne mansion. The house contains fine collections of
furniture, porcelain and paintings and is set in the peaceful
tranquillity of sixty-six acres of formal gardens, unique in the
British Isles for their 'grand vista' design inspired by Andre le
Nôtre who created Versailles. They remain as they were
originally laid over 250 years ago with ornamental ponds,
cascades, tall beech hedges and loggias of various shapes.
The gardens are noted for the magnificent display of daffodils
and other spring flowers. Throughout the summer a fine
display of flowers of infinite variety vie with the roses for
your enjoyment. Three long vistas stretch into the Pleasure
Grounds of Black Fen where in the more natural and wilder
habitat nature trails have been established amongst the
magnificent cedar, copper beech and Spanish chestnut rides
radiating from temples and an obelisk.

Open: Gardens: Saturday to Monday, Easter Mayday and
Spring Bank Holiday. House and Gardens: Sundays,
Tuesdays, Wednesdays and Thursdays from 14th June to 31st
August. Open 1.15 p.m. – 5.30 p.m. (last admission 5 p.m.).

Admission: House and Gardens – Adults: £3; Children: £1; Senior Citizens: £1.50. Grounds Only – Adults: £2; Children: 50p; Senior Citizens: £1. Reduced admission rates for parties of twenty or more

Facilities: Car park, coach park (in stable yard).

Disabled Access: Toilets and ramp to gardens only.

Additional Information: Dogs on leash in gardens, picnics in gardens.

BROUGHTON CASTLE

Broughton Castle, Banbury, Oxon, OX15 5EB.
(0295) 262624

Ownership: Lord Saye & Sele.

Status: Privately owned.

General Description: Castle built in 1300 and greatly enlarged in 1550. Surrounded by a three acre moat and standing on a three acre island. Has been in the ownership of the family for over 600 years. The garden features magnificent borders, a walled 'ladies garden' and beds of old fashioned roses.

Open: 20th May – 13th September, Wednesdays and Sundays also Thursdays in July and August and Bank Holiday Sundays and Bank Holiday Mondays (including Easter).

Admission: Adults: £2.80; Senior Citizens/Students: £2.10; Children: £1.40.

Facilities: Car park, tea room, shop.

Disabled Access: To ground floor of house and gardens.

Additional Information: Picnics in the park, dogs allowed in park and garden.

BRYMPTON HOUSE AND GARDENS

Brympton d'Evercy, Yeovil, Somerset, BA22 8TD.
(0935) 862528 or 86247

Ownership: Charles E. B. Clive-Ponsonby-Fane.

Status: Private.

General Description: 'I know of no other house where the whole impression is more lovely and none that summarises so exquisitely the best of English Country Life' wrote Christopher in *Country Life* magazine. The gardens, created by Judy Clive-Ponsonby-Fane, are designed not only to be of interest in themselves but to compliment and enhance the magnificent range of Vernacular buildings, so much so that she was presented the 'Garden of the Year Award'. Alongside the House, the Brympton vineyard has been established and produces in excess of 2,000 bottles of English white wine every year. In the museum, Britain's smallest legal distillery now produces Brympton Apple Brandy from a mobile still, imported from the Calvados region of France. Throughout the summer there are exhibitions of photographs and water colours in the old stables gallery.

Open: Easter Friday to Monday (inclusive) and then May to September (inclusive) every afternoon 2 p.m. – 6 p.m. (Except Fridays for 1992).

Admission: House, gardens, museum and exhibitions: Adult: £3.90; Child: £1.50. Discounts for parties, Senior Citizens and National Trust members.

Facilities: Free parking, freshly made teas and cream teas.

Disabled Access: Easy access, ramps, special toilets.

Additional Information: Dogs welcome to be exercised on cricket ground but not in gardens.

BURFORD HOUSE GARDENS

Tenbury Wells, Worcestershire, WR15 8HQ.
(0584) 810777

Ownership: Treasures of Tenbury Ltd.

Status: Independent.

General Description: Burford House Gardens are situated in unusually fine scenery, flanked on the one side by the River Teme and its tributary, with the Bednall hills rising steeply to the south. Apart from the extensive lawns, the gardens contain a vast collection of plants acquired by John Treasure during the last thirty-five years. The gardens never fail to have some point of interest throughout the seasons of the year, from the scents and colours of high summer to the warm glowing tones of autumn. The adjoining newly designed Plant Centre specialises in clematis and herbaceous plants, including many plants seen in the gardens.

Open: March to October: Monday to Saturday, 10 a.m. – 5 p.m., Sunday 1 p.m. – 5 p.m.

Admission: Adults: £1.95; Children: 80p; Parties (twenty-five or more): £1.60 each.

Facilities: Free parking, tearooms.

Disabled Access: Access for disabled visitors to all areas, disabled toilets available.

Additional Information: Dogs not allowed in gardens. Nature reserve and adventure playground planned for 1992.

BURNBY HALL GARDENS AND MUSEUM

The Balk, Pocklington, Humberside.
(0759) 302068

Ownership: Stewarts Gardens and Museum Trust.

General Description: Major P. M. Stewart commenced the construction of the concrete lined lakes in 1905 and devoted a large part of his life to landscaping the Gardens and maintaining the large collection of water lilies. On his death in 1962 a Trust was formed to carry on in his tradition. The two lakes covering approximately two acres contain the National collection of water lilies (Age Concern Award Winner, 1991) along with a large variety of fish. Rose garden and herbaceous borders lead to pleasant walks by the waterfall through the rockery to lakeside paths and a tree shaded walk. The free Museum houses a unique collection of ethnic and sporting trophies from the Mayor's many travels around the world.

Open: Easter to mid October (weather permitting) 10 a.m. – 6 p.m. – last admission 5.15 p.m.

Admission: Adults: £1.50; Senior Citizens £1; Parties over twenty: £1; Children: (5-16): 50p; Under 5's: free.

Facilities: Free car/coach parking, cafe, sales kiosk.

Disabled Access: Toilets, special area nearer to gardens for parking, wheelchairs available (free).

Additional Information: Large picnic area and benches, seats around the lakes, only guide dogs allowed.

CASTLE ASHBY GARDENS

Castle Ashby, Northampton, NN7 1LQ.
(060) 129 234

Ownership: The Marquess of Northampton.

Status: Privately owned.

General Description: Castle Ashby is a fascinating combination of eighteenth- and nineteenth-century gardening styles. Both formal gardens and parkland have recently undergone considerable restoration. An extensive tree planting programme has been carried out in the parkland, based on 'Capability' Brown's original plan of 1761. The Terrace Gardens have now been returned to their original layout and once again complement the impressive Elizabethan house. A short distance from the house can be found the Italian Gardens and Arboretum. Here the mood is more intimate and tranquil. Formal ponds, terracotta vases and topiary unite a design which is dominated by a series of nineteenth-century glasshouses. The most impressive of these is the Conservatory which was completely replanted in 1986. The Arboretum contains some superb mature trees, while the grassland underneath is managed as a hay meadow to encourage both native wild flowers and the wide range of flowering bulbs for which the gardens are renowned.

Open: Daily 10 a.m. – 6 p.m. Occasional closures for events, house tours for parties by appointment.

Admission: Adults: £1; Children/Senior Citizens: 50p. Tickets from machine when car park not attended, coach parties by arrangement.

Facilities: Car park in village, shops and tearoom in farmyard.

Disabled Access: Most areas suitable for wheelchair users.

Additional Information: Terrace gardens can be viewed but are not open to the public, dogs allowed on leads, picnics possible.

CASTLE DROGO

Drewsteignton, Exeter, Devon, EX6 6PB.
(0647) 433306

Ownership: The National Trust.

Status: The National Trust.

General Description: Perched on a crag overlooking the Teign Gorge the castle is a marvel of the ingenuity of the architect Sir Edwin Lutyens. It was built between 1910 splendours of a medieval fortress with the opulent luxuries required by the Drewe family, including its own hydroelectric and telephone systems. The secluded garden features a series of formal terraces and herbaceous borders leading to a magnificent circular lawn surrounded by a tall yew hedge. There are magnificent views of the wooded gorge of the Teign to Dartmoor beyond.

Open: 1st April to 1st November, 11 a.m. – 5.30 p.m. (last admission 5 p.m.).

Admission: Castle and Grounds: £4.40, Grounds only: £2; Children (5-16 years): half price.

Facilities: Car park, counter service tearoom, waitress service restaurant, shop, croquet lawn with equipment for hire.

Disabled Access: Limited access to castle, access to garden, restaurant etc. Toilets at visitor reception.

Additional Information: No dogs in castle or immediate surroundings.

CASTLE HOWARD

York YO6 7DA.
(065) 384 333

Ownership: The Hon. Simon Howard.

Status: Member of the Historic Houses Association.

General Description: This eighteenth-century house designed by John Vanbrugh the finest private residence in Yorkshire, begun in 1699 for Charles Howard, the third Earl of Carlisle is still the home of the Howard family. Its many rooms show collections of antique furniture, porcelain and sculpture, whilst its important paintings represent the art of masters such as Rubens, Reynolds, Gainsborough and Holbein. The Costume Galleries show displays of historical costume. There are two rose gardens, one featuring old roses and the other modern varieties. Way Wood was opened to the public for the first time in 1990. This is a unique collection of rare trees, shrubs, rhododendrons and azaleas by James Russell, Arboretum Curator.

Open: From 25th March to 1st November every day. The Grounds and Gardens open at 10 a.m., the House and Galleries at 11 a.m. Last admissions are 4.30 p.m.

Admission: Adults: £3.50; Children: £1.50.

Facilities: Car and coach parking free of charge. There is a self service cafeteria. The Lakeside cafeteria is open during the summer months.

Disabled Access: There is disabled parking and toilets. Most wheelchair visitors can see all areas which are open to the public with the exception of the Chapel.

Additional Information: Picnics are permitted in the grounds, dogs are welcome in the grounds but must be kept on leads. There is an excellent Plant Centre selling a range of plants and garden accessories. There are two adventure playgrounds.

CHARTWELL

Westerham, Kent, TN16 1PS.
(0732) 866368

Ownership: National Trust.

Status: National Trust.

General Description: Home of Sir Winston Churchill
from 1924 the house, garden and studio evoke his career and
interests. In the garden stands the wall he built incorporating
a Wendy House for his daughter. The garden is on several
levels with terraces overlooking the High Weald. In pools on
the higher level swim the Golden Orfe Sir Winston enjoyed
feeding and a series of other pools with waterfalls lead down
to the circular swimming pool. At the lowest level the garden
is bounded by a long lake at the end of which there is a statue
of Sir Winston and Lady Churchill, by Oscar Nemon. The
colour in the garden is provided by herbaceous borders below
the terraces and two formal rose gardens. A feeling of great
space is given by lawns which sweep down the hillside
towards the lake.

Open: House only: March and November: Saturday, Sunday
and Wednesday, 11 a.m. – 4.30 p.m. House, Garden and
Studio: April to end October: Tuesday, Wednesday,
Thursday, 12 p.m. – 5.30 p.m. Saturday Sunday, Bank
Holiday Monday, 11 a.m. – 5.30 p.m. last admission half
hour before closing. Closed Good Friday and Tuesday
following Bank Holiday Monday. Timed tickets in operation.

Admission: House only (March to November) – Adult: £2.30; Child: £1.20. House and Garden – Adult: £3.80, Child: £1.90. Garden only – Adult: £1.60; Child: 80p. Studio 50p extra. Pre-booked parties (Tuesday morning): Adult: £3.10; Child: £1.60.

Facilities: Restaurant open March and November 10.30 a.m. – 4 p.m. April to end October 10.30 a.m. – 5 p.m. on days house is open. Licensed (no spirits). Shop open same times as house, picnic area next to car park, dogs on leads allowed in garden only.

Disabled Access: The garden is hilly, with some steep paths and flights of steps. Telephone the administrator in advance for special parking. The ground floor to the house is accessible. There is a small lift to the first floor. Toilets for wheelchair users in coach park near restaurant.

Additional Information: Picnic area near car park., dogs allowed in garden on leads, information kiosk in car park, no photography in the house.

CHATSWORTH

Bakewell, Derbyshire, DE4 1PP.
(0246) 582204

Ownership: Chatsworth House Trust.

Status: Privately owned.

General Description: The garden covers over 100 acres. It
provides many delights and surprises: a cascade, spectacular
fountains and rocks, a tropical greenhouse, herbaceous
borders, rose garden and secluded walks among rare shrubs
and forest trees. The surrounding park of 1,000 acres was
landscaped by 'Capability' Brown. Open for the first time in
1992 is the newly laid out Kitchen Garden. Accessible for
wheelchairs. A brass band will play in the Garden on Sunday
afternoons throughout June, July and August.

Open: Every day from April to the end of October, 11.30
a.m. – 4.30 p.m.

Admission: Adults: £4.75; Senior Citizens: £4; Children:
£2.25. Reductions for groups who book in advance.

Facilities: Unlimited parking for cars and coaches, fully
licensed restaurant, gift shops, baby room, coach drivers' rest
room.

Disabled Access: No admittance to house due to the number
of stairs but garden, restaurant and shops accessible and
disabled toilet facilities, a special leaflet for disabled visitors
is available on arrival.

Additional Information: Dogs allowed in the garden on a
lead, special events take place in the park throughout the
year, visitors are welcome to picnic anywhere in the garden
or the park. A brass band plays in the garden on Sunday
afternoons in June, July and August.

CLAREMONT LANDSCAPE GARDEN

Esher, Surrey, KT10 9JG.
(0372) 469421

Ownership: The National Trust, Garden only.

Status: The National Trust.

General Description: One of the earliest surviving English landscape gardens restored by National Trust, begun by Sir John Vanbrugh and Charles Bridgeman before 1720, extended and naturalised by William Kent, 'Capability' Brown also made improvements. Lake, island with pavilion, grotto, turf amphitheatre, viewpoints and avenues.

Open: All year daily: March, 10 a.m. – 5 p.m., April to end October, Monday to Friday, 10 a.m. – 6 p.m., Saturday, Sunday and Bank Holidays, 10 a.m. – 7 p.m. (15th to 19th July garden closes at 4 p.m.). November to end March, daily (excluding Mondays), 10 a.m. – 5 p.m. or sunset if earlier. Closed 25th December and 1st January.

Admission: Sundays and Bank Holiday Mondays: £2.50; Monday to Saturday: £1.50; Children under 17 years: £1.25; Under 5's: free. No reduction for parties.

Facilities: Tearoom and shop open March, Saturday and Sunday, 11 a.m. – 4.30 p.m. April to end October, daily (except Monday), 11 a.m. – 5.30 p.m. November to 13th December daily (except Monday) 11 a.m. – 4.30 p.m. (Tearoom closes 4 p.m.). 16th January to end March 1993 Saturday and Sunday 11 a.m. – 4.30 p.m. Open Bank Holiday Mondays.

Disabled Access: Level pathway around lake and level grassland, disabled toilets in car park.

Additional Information: Picnics permitted, no dogs in garden between 1st April and 1st November, dogs allowed November to end March.

COMPTON ACRES GARDENS

Canford Cliffs Road, Poole, Dorset, BH13 7ES.
(0202) 700778

Status: Privately owned.

General Description: The story of Compton Acres starts
about 1919, when the late T. W. Simpson conceived the idea.
It took several years of planning and expenditure before the
gardens evolved. Rare plants, many tropical and sub-tropical,
together with a priceless collection of bronze and marble
statuary, lead figures and vases, were collected from all over
the world. The Japanese garden is reputed to be the only
completely genuine Japanese garden in Europe. Equally
delightful are the Italian garden, rock and water gardens, the
woodland walk and glen, heather and Roman gardens, and
palm court. An exciting new collection of magnificent
sculptures has been introduced to the gardens.

Open: 1st March to end October 10.30 a.m. – 6.30 p.m. daily.
Last admission 5.45 p.m.

Admission: Adults: £3.30; Senior Citizens/Students: £2.40;
Children: £1; Group rates available.

Facilities: Large car and coach park, cafeteria, creperie and
non-alcoholic wine bar, gift shop, and garden centre.

Disabled Access: Paths throughout the gardens avoiding
steps, ramps into shops and cafeteria, disabled toilets.

Additional Information: No picnic area, but there are
benches within the gardens, no radios, no dogs (only guide
dogs).

CORSHAM COURT

Corsham, Wilts, SN13 0BX.
(0249) 712214

Ownership: Lord Methuen Arics.

Status: Historic Houses Association.

General Description: Corsham Court stands in a secluded, mature and spacious garden. Designed by 'Capability' Brown and later completed by Repton. It is worth a visit at any time of year, especially resplendent in spring with magnolias, daffodils and later, syringas. There are lovely plants and specimen trees, lawns, lily pond and a formal rose garden. Corsham Court contains a famous collection of paintings by Old Masters along with other treasures.

Open: Staterooms 1st January to 30th November daily (not Mondays and Fridays) 2 p.m. – 4 p.m. (From Good Friday to 30th September 2 p.m. – 6 p.m. (including Friday and Bank Holidays). (Closed December). Other times by appointment. Parties welcome.

Admission: House and Gardens – Adult: £3; Child: £1.50 (Parties of twenty or more by arrangement). Gardens only – Adults: £1.50; Child: £1.

Facilities: Free parking.

Disabled Access: Disabled toilets.

Additional Information: Picnic in garden, dogs on leads in garden.

COTEHELE

St. Dominick, near Saltash, Cornwall, PL12 6TA.
(0579) 50434

Status: National Trust.

General Description: Cotehele House, built by the
Edgcumbe family in the late fifteenth century, stands at the
head of a steep valley with woodland sheltering the valley
garden. Exotic and tender plants, such as palms, ferns and
Gunnera manicata, thrive in the mild climate. Fine display of
azaleas. Further down the valley are spruces, hemlocks and
larches. Garden contains the medieval stewpond, now filled
with water-lilies, and a domed dovecote. Areas of garden
surrounding the house are more formal. Nineteenth-century
terraces with roses and magnolias to the east of the house.
North-west of the house is a meadow with Judas trees and
daffodils.

Open: 1st April to 1st November daily, except Friday when
the house only is closed (but open Good Friday), October –
11 a.m. – 5.30 p.m., closes 5 p.m. in October. Last admission
half hour before closing.

Admission: £4.80; Grounds: £2.40; Party bookings: £4.00.

Facilities: Restaurant, shop, toilets.

Disabled Access: Gardens unsuitable for wheelchairs due to
steep slopes and gravel paths, disabled toilets, guide dogs
admitted.

COTON MANOR GARDENS

Coton, near Guilsborough, Northamptonshire.
(0604) 740219

Ownership: Mr. and Mrs. Ian Pasley-Tyler.

General Description: The gardens are located in superb rural countryside. Although established in the early part of this century, the gardens, covering some ten acres, embody many of the features associated with a traditional old English garden. Being situated on a hillside they are exquisitely laid out on different levels and comprise herbaceous borders, with a wealth of unusual plants, lakes, water gardens, old hedges and lawns. The charm is enhanced by flamingoes, cranes and waterfowl roaming at large providing added interest and appeal for gardeners and nature lovers alike.

Open: Easter to end of September, Wednesdays, Sunday and Bank Holiday Mondays, also Thursdays in July and August.

Admission: Adult: £2.50; Senior Citizens: £2; Children: 50p.

Facilities: Free car park, tearoom, gift shop.

Disabled Access: Gardens fully accessible for wheelchair users.

Additional Information: Picnics are permitted in the car park, dogs allowed on leads.

CRAGSIDE HOUSE AND COUNTRY PARK

Rothbury, Morpeth, Northumberland, NE65 7PX.
House: (0669) 20333; Country Park: (0669) 21051

Ownership: The National Trust.

Status: The National Trust.

General Description: The Cragside estate consists of 950 acres of pleasure grounds. The house built from 1863 onwards is surrounded by a magnificent three and a half acre rock garden, sweeping down to the Debdon Valley with its waterfalls and pools. The pinetum in the valley has a fine collection of conifers from mainly North America but not exclusively. The country park is based on the Himalayan rhododendron forests and planted with nineteenth-century rhododendrons and azaleas. The formal garden consists of an Italian garden, rose loggia, orchard glasshouse, thirty-six acres of park land, fine collection of hollies in clipped form and a fine conifer collection.

Open: Country Park: daily, 1st April to 31st October, 10.30 a.m. – 7 p.m. Winter weekends, 10.30 a.m. – 4 p.m. House 1st April to October, 1 p.m. – 5.30 p.m.

Admission: House and Country Park (including gardens): £5; Children: half price; Country Park only (including gardens): £3.20.

Facilities: Parking, toilets, restaurant, energy centre, power house, ram house, video of estate's history, computer game on energy, shop, ice cream, fishing and picnic areas.

Disabled Access: Disabled toilets and parking, access difficult in steep sloping garden areas, six mile car driveway and viewing points around the estate.

Additional Information: Picnic area around estate, dogs on lead in rock garden and Debdon Valley, no dogs allowed in the formal garden.

CROFT CASTLE

Leominster, Hereford and Worcester, HR6 9PW.
(0568) 85 246

Ownership: The National Trust.

Status: National Trust.

General Description: The four round corner towers and
ancient walls date from the fourteenth or fifteenth century;
inside, the fine Georgian Gothic staircase and ceilings were
added in the eighteenth century. Family portraits and
interesting furniture, including a fine collection of Georgian
chairs in the Gothic taste. The park contains exceptional
avenues of Spanish chestnut (400 years old), oak and beech
and an Iron Age fort from which fourteen counties can be
seen on a clear day.

Open: April and October: Saturday and Sunday: 2 p.m. –
5 p.m., Easter Saturday, Sunday and Monday, 2 p.m. –
6 p.m., May to end September, Wednesday to Sunday and
Bank Holiday Monday, 2 p.m. – 6 p.m. Last admissions half
hour before closing.

Admission: Adult: £2.70; Family Ticket: £7.40.

Facilities: Free car parking.

Disabled Access: Access to ground floor only and part of
grounds, special parking by castle.

Additional Information: Dogs in parkland on leads only,
picnics welcome in parkland only.

DALEMAIN

Dalemain, Penrith, Cumbria, CA11 0HB.
(07684) 86450

Ownership: Dalemain Estates.

Status: Historic Houses Association.

General Description: The Garden at Dalemain has a long history stretching back to the medieval Herb Garden. In the sixteenth century the Walled Garden enclosed borders filled with Tudor roses and a charming gazebo or 'grotto'. The walls were substantially enlarged first in the 1680's by Sir Edward Hasell and then by his son in the 1740's leaving the layout much as the visitor will find it today. The imposing terrace wall reaches from the side of the mansion back into the garden and supports a full and colourful herbaceous border during the summer months. Mrs. McCosh has in recent years revitalised the gardens, replacing many of the borders, introducing rare and exotic plants.

Open: Sunday to Thursday, 19th April to 4th October, 11.15 a.m. – 5 p.m.

Admission: Gardens only – Adult: £2.50; Children: free; Disabled visitors free.

Facilities: Car park, tearoom serving afternoon teas.

Disabled Access: Disabled toilets, access to gardens.

Additional Information: Picnic tables, no dogs except guide dogs.

DYRHAM PARK

Dyrham, near Chippenham, Wiltshire, SN14 8ER.
(027582) 2501

Ownership: The National Trust.

Status: The National Trust.

General Description: At the foot of 263 acres of ancient parkland grazed by fallow deer and looking across to the Welsh hills is William Blathwayt's magnificent mansion. Little has changed in the rooms at Dyrham since Blathwayt furnished them and the content was recorded in his housekeeper's inventory. The house is a marvellous reminder of the seventeenth century. The park is an outstanding example of English landscape gardening.

Open: House, Garden and Park – 1st April to 1st November daily except Thursdays and Fridays, 12 p.m. – 5.30 p.m. Park only – all year daily 12 a.m. – 5.30 p.m. (closed Christmas Day).

Admission: £4.40; or park only £1.40.

Facilities: Restaurant and shop.

Disabled Access: Suitable for disabled and visually handicapped visitors.

Additional Information: No dogs.

EMMETTS GARDEN

Ide Hill, Kent.
(073 275) 367 or 429

Ownership: The National Trust.

Status: The National Trust.

General Description: The garden covers five acres and is thought to be the highest garden in Kent. Emmetts Garden is a delightful garden, ablaze with colour during May and June, with azaleas and rhododendrons. A magnificent 100 feet Wellingtonia stands next to the Victorian mansion (not open to the public), and is the tallest tree top in Kent. Emmetts was acquired by the National Trust in 1965 and much restoration work has been done, including a rock garden which was discovered by chance by the Head Gardener. There are many unusual trees and shrubs and a wonderful bluebell bank. This is a much loved garden, which people return to again and again.

Open: April to end October, Wednesday to Sunday and Bank Holiday Monday 2 p.m. – 6 p.m. (last admission 5 p.m.).

Admission: Adults: £2.20; Children: £1.10.

Facilities: Tearoom, 2 p.m. – 5 p.m. same days as garden.

Disabled Access: Most of garden suitable, golf buggy available from car park to ticket hut.

Additional Information: Dogs allowed on leads, annual two-day country fair and dozens of stands and attractions.

EXBURY GARDENS

Exbury, Southampton, Hampshire.
(0703) 897181.

Ownership: Exbury Gardens Trust.

General Description: This 200 acre landscaped woodland
garden is renowned for its collection of rhododendrons,
azaleas, magnolias and camellias, built up by the de
Rothschild family since the 1920s. The gardens, which lie on
the east bank of the Beaulieu River, contain many interesting
features to enhance the colourful spring flowering displays
and the more tranquil atmosphere of summer and autumn. As
well as many notable trees and shrubs, the visitor can enjoy
countless walks, the rock garden, water gardens, the recently
restored iris garden, heather gardens, ponds and cascades and
daffodil meadow. At the garden's entrance there is a gift shop
and plant centre where expert advice is available. Both of
these remain open throughout the year. Also there are two
licensed tearooms where hot and cold lunches and cream teas
are served. An artist's gallery contains remarkable paintings
by Exbury's 'resident artist'.

Open: 29th February to mid April – Adult: £2.50; Senior
Citizens: £2; Parties (fifteen or more): £2; Child: £1.50. Mid
April to mid June – Adult: £3.50; Senior Citizens: £3;
Parties: £3; Child: £2.50. Mid June to 5th July – Adult:
£2.50; Senior Citizens: £2; Parties: £2; Child: £1.50.

Senior Citizens: £1; Parties: £1.50; Child: £1.

* 53 acre Summer Garden.

Autumn – 5th September to 25th October – Adult: £2; Senior
Citizens: £1.50; Parties: £1.50; Child: £1.

Children under 10 free.

Facilities: Free parking, two licensed tea rooms serving hot
and cold lunches and cream teas.

Disabled Access: Disabled toilets, tracks mainly level but
some unsuitable hence signed wheelchair route.

Additional Information: Dogs welcome on short leads,
picnic area.

FELBRIGG HALL

Roughton, Norwich, Norfolk, NR11 8PR.
(026375) 44

Ownership: The National Trust.

Status: National Trust.

General Description: One of the finest seventeenth-century houses in Norfolk, with its original eighteenth-century furniture and pictures (Grand Tour and Family Portraits) and an outstanding library; walled garden, including a restored dovecote, has a traditional layout of herbaceous plants and fruit trees; walks in fine, mature woodland and around lake.

Open: 28th March to 1st November, Monday, Wednesday, Thursday, Saturday, Sunday. Garden 11 a.m. – 5.30 p.m. Hall 1.30 p.m. – 5.30 p.m. Park and Woodland, all year, dawn to dusk.

Admission: Hall and Garden: £4.30; Garden only: £1.60 (children £2 and 80p). Park and Woodland, free.

Facilities: Ample parking, restaurant daily April to end October, shop same as Hall, toilets, baby room.

Disabled Access: Electric buggy for garden, braille guides – Hall, garden, woodland and lakeside walk, easy access ground floor of Hall, restaurant and shop, wheelchairs available.

Additional Information: Picnic site 300 yards past Hall, dogs on lead in woodland and parkland.

FORDE ABBEY AND GARDENS

Chard, Somerset ,TA20 4LU.
(0460) 20231

Ownership: Trustees of Mr. Mark Roper.

Status: Historic Houses Association.

General Description: Thirty acres of gardens surround this great building. The top lake is probably monastic but the earliest garden work dates from the early eighteenth century. Several views remain from the early plantings. The garden is informal, there are four lakes and many outstanding trees among the shrubberies. Spring bulbs do particularly well in the acid, gravelly soil. Herbaceous borders, sheltered by old stone and brick walls are a feature of this garden. In the Bog Garden will be found a large collection of moisture loving plants, including primulas, meconopis and iris among many others. Great new plantings have recently taken place in the Rock Garden. The transformation has been supervised by a retired alpine nurseryman of world renown! To the east of the garden are six acres of Arboretum planted since 1945. At the back of the Abbey is a working kitchen garden, also a nursery that requires the close attention of keen gardeners.

Open: Gardens, open daily throughout year 10 a.m. – 4.30 p.m. Abbey, 1st April to end October, 1 p.m. – 4.30 p.m. last admission on Sunday, Wednesday and Bank Holidays. Special private tour of Abbey may be arranged on Monday, Tuesday, Wednesday a.m. Thursday and Friday.

Admission: Gardens only – Coaches: £2.60; Adult: £3;
Senior Citizens £2.60. Abbey and Garden – Coaches: £3.30;
Adult: £4.30; Senior Citizens: £3.80. Private Tours – Under
fifty persons: £4.30; over fifty persons: £3.80. Children
accompanied by Adult: under 15 free.

Facilities: Parking free, self-service restaurant in twelfth-
century undercroft. Access to garden and hall but not to
abbey. Free entry to garden for wheelchair users.

Disabled Access: Garden and toilets fine, Abbey not
accessible, except hall, disabled persons may look into hall
from garden. In wheelchairs, entry to garden free.

Additional Information: Controlled dogs on lead allowed in
garden, not in Abbey, picnics allowed in garden.

GLENDURGAN GARDEN

Helford River, Mawnan Smith, near Falmouth, Cornwall, TR11 5JZ.
(0208) 74281

Ownership: National Trust.

Status: The National Trust.

General Description: Delightful and informal garden at head
of steep valley leading to Helford River. Warm, wet and
sheltered site. Garden originally planned by Alfred Fox,
owner of prosperous local shipping company in 1820s and
1830s who planted garden with exotic plants brought back
from the Americas, Africa, Far East and the Antipodes.
Planted laurel maze and probably the two tulip trees which
are over 150 years old. Next two generations of the family
expanded the garden and planted many trees including
cedars, weeping spruce, and cypresses. Rhododendrons,
camellias and hydrangeas provide colour as do the carpets of
primroses, bluebells, primulas and columbines beneath the
trees in spring. A Holy Corner is planted with trees and
shrubs with Biblical associations – a yew, tree of thorns and
tree of heaven.

Open: 1st March to 31st October Tuesdays to Saturday (not
Good Friday) but open Bank Holiday Mondays, 10.30 a.m. –
5.30 p.m. last admission 4.30 p.m.

Admission: £2.50.

Facilities: Toilets.

Disabled Access: Garden slopes steeply so unsuitable for
wheelchairs, guide dogs admitted.

GREAT DIXTER HOUSE AND GARDENS

Northiam, East Sussex, TN31 6PH.
(0797) 253160

Ownership: The Lloyd family.

Status: Historic Houses Association, Europa Northern.

General Description: The Manor of Dixter is first mentioned
in 1220, but the oldest part of the present structure, the Great
Hall, dates from about 1450–64. Mr. Nathaniel Lloyd bought
it in 1910 and entrusted the restoration, addition and design
of the gardens to Sir Edwin Lutyens. These were completed
before the First World War. The gardens are laid out on the
site of the farm yards and many of the original farm buildings
have been retained in the design. The three kiln oasthouse
was last used for drying hops in 1939. Mr. Lloyd designed
and constructed the sunk garden with octagonal pool in 1923.
The illustration above is from his bookplate. The House is of
three ages. The porch and to the right is the original building
of the mid-fifteenth century. This part is open to the public.
Floors and dividing partitions inserted in about 1595 were
removed by Lutyens who designed the new domestic
accommodation which extends from the porch to the left. At
the back is attached a mid-fifteenth century yeoman's hall
house which Mr. Lloyd found standing in a derelict site in
Benenden.

Open: 1st April to 11th October and 17th/18th and 24th/25th
October, Tuesday to Sundays and Public Holidays 2 p.m. –
5 p.m. (last admission).

Admission: House and Gardens: £3.20; Children: 50p; Gardens only: £2; Children: 25p.

Facilities: Parking, teas.

Additional Information: Picnic in two car parks, good views, no dogs.

HADDON HALL

Bakewell, Derbyshire, DE4 1LA.
(0629) 812855

Ownership: His Grace The Duke of Rutland C.B.E.

Status: Private, but member of Historic Houses Association.

General Description: The gardens at Haddon Hall cascade, in seven terraces, down a steep hillside to the River Wye. Noted, in particular, for the astonishing collection of Old English rambling roses and clematis, the garden is planted to provide year round colour, early shows of massed narcissi and tulips of sixty varieties, are followed by the early climbing roses, which embrace the building. The house and gardens, were abandoned during the 1700s and 1800s, but were meticulously returned earlier this century to recreate the charm of this perfect English country garden.

Open: 1st April to 30th September, 11 a.m. – 6 p.m. daily, except Monday. Also closed Sundays in July and August.

Admission: Adults: £3.20; Senior Citizens: £2.60; Party Rate: £2.60; Children: £1.90, no separate admission for gardens.

Facilities: Car park (50p), self-service restaurant, gift shop.

Additional Information: No dogs, picnics allowed in the grounds, photography is welcomed in house and gardens.

HAREWOOD HOUSE

Harewood, Leeds, West Yorkshire, LS17 9LQ.
(0532) 886225

Ownership: The Rt. Hon. The Earl of Harewood.

Status: Privately owned.

General Description: Harewood House – home of the Earl and Countess of Harewood – was built and designed by John Carr and Robert Adam. The eighteenth-century house contains rare Sevres and Chinese porcelain, English and Italian paintings and superb furniture by Thomas Chippendale. Harewood Bird Garden covers four and a half acres and contains over 170 species of birds from all over the world. The refurbished Tropical House simulates Rain Forest conditions with birds and plants in their natural environments. Lakeside and Terrace Ornamental Gardens add to the splendour of Harewood, making it a true House of England.

Open: 5th April to 31st October, daily, 10 a.m. – 7 p.m.

Admission: Gardens: £2, additional charge to House or/and Bird Garden.

Facilities: Ample parking, coffee shop, private function suite, study centre, gift shops, large adventure playground.

Disabled Access: Good access for wheelchair users although some areas on incline, disabled toilet facilities.

Additional Information: Dogs allowed but must be kept on lead at all times, very large picnic and play areas.

HATFIELD HOUSE

Hatfield, Hertfordshire, AL9 5NQ.
(0707) 262823

Ownership: The Marquess of Salisbury.

Status: Private ownership.

General Description: The West Gardens of the house date back to the late fifteenth century, and were created by Robert Cecil, 1st Earl of Salisbury, and planted by John Tradescant the Elder. In the last years (and the work is still continuing) the present Marchioness has tried to re-create the Gardens, as far as possible, in their planting and design to have the feeling and manner of gardens in the seveteenth century, in sympathy with the Great House. There is a Formal Garden, enclosed by a yew hedge and its design is copied from an early plan found in the archives. Below it is a Scented Garden with a Herb Garden at its centre.

Open: 25th March to 11th October. 11 a.m. – 6 p.m. every day. East Gardens 2 p.m. – 5 p.m. Mondays, not Bank Holidays.

Admission: Adults: £2.40; Senior Citizens: £2.20; Children: £1.80. Parties (twenty plus booked in advance) – Adults: £2.20; Children: £1.60.

Facilities: Ample parking including coaches, restaurant, venture play area, nature trails in park, gift and garden shops.

Disabled Access: Disabled toilets, most of gardens accessible to wheelchair users.

Additional Information: Outside and inside picnic facilities, dogs allowed in park but not in house or gardens.

HELMINGHAM HALL GARDENS

Helmingham, Stowmarket, Suffolk, IP14 6EF.
(0473) 890363

Ownership: The Lord Tollemache.

Status: English Heritage, Historic Houses Association.

General Description: Helmingham and its Gardens have
been the home of the Tollemache family since 1480 when
they built the Hall, surrounding it with a wide moat (the
drawbridges are still raised every night). There is a large
walled kitchen garden, the eight beds of which are divided by
magnificent herbaceous borders and arches of gourds, runner
beans and sweet peas. On the other side of the Hall there is a
Knot Garden which also contains a large collection of old
fashioned roses and other unusual plants. The whole is set in
400 acres of ancient Deer Park with a herd of 500 red and
fallow deer.

Open: Every Sunday between 2 p.m. and 6 p.m. from 3rd
May to 13th September. In addition, parties of thirty
(minimum) welcome on Wednesday afternoons during the
above opening dates – by prior appointment.

Admission: Adults: £2; Senior Citizens: £1.80; Children (15
and under): £1.10. Safari rides – Adults: 80p; Children: 60p.

Facilities: Ample free parking, coach house tearooms, gift
shop, home grown produce for sale.

Disabled Access: Accessible, no steps.

Additional Information: Dogs allowed on leads, picnic areas.

HERGEST CROFT GARDENS

Kington, Herefordshire, HR5 3EG.
(0544) 230160

Ownership: Mr. W. L. Banks.

Status: Private ownership.

General Description: In a secluded valley amid an ancient
oakwood a corner of the Himalayas has been created with an
astonishing variety of rhododendrons. The parkland, grazed
by sheep, is planted with trees seldom seen outside a botanic
garden. At the heart of it all are two gardens full of beauty
and interest at any season. The garden surrounding Hergest
Croft has magnolias in May, azaleas in May and June, lilies,
roses, hydrangeas in July and August and vivid autumn
colour from the National Collection of maples and birches.
The kitchen garden has much besides fruit and vegetables.
There is an apple avenue carpeted with rare bulbs and
unusual primroses in spring, magnificent double herbaceous
borders and old fashioned roses in summer. There is a
fascinating range of wild birds from buzzard to tree creeper
and a well labelled collection of plants.

Open: 17th April to 25th October daily 1.30 p.m. – 6.30 p.m.

Admission: Adult: £2; Season: £8; Children under 15 free.
Adults in parties of twenty or over: £1.50.

Facilities: Parking, toilets, tearoom, shop – rare plants for
sale.

Disabled Access: Access, but terrain not easy.

Additional Information: Dogs on leads allowed, picnics
allowed but no special arrangements made.

HESTERCOMBE GARDENS

Cheddon Fitzpaine, Taunton, Somerset, TA2 8LQ.
(0823) 337222

Ownership: Somerset County Council.

General Description: The gardens are the work of the world famous partnership of Sir Edwin Lutyens and Miss Gertrude Jekyll. They are terraced into a south facing hillside, thus affording a place to grow many mediterranean plants. The borders have been faithfully restored to Miss Jekyll's original planting plans, using the many roses, shrubs and herbaceous plants she used in the early 1900s. The garden strongly reflects Lutyens' bold geometric designs, the pavings and recently restored pools and water channels and pergola, giving a unique framework on which to work the subtle tapestry of the planting scheme. The garden is at its best as a whole in May to September. The garden has been restored by Somerset Fire Brigade and is maintained by them as part of the Headquarters' complex. This quiet garden is said to be the pinnacle of the Lutyens and Jekyll collaboration and is truly a garden of the Edwardian era.

Open: All year, Monday to Friday 9 a.m. – 5 p.m. 1st May to 3rd September, Saturdays and Sundays, 2 p.m. – 5 p.m.

Admission: £1.

Facilities: Car parking free, toilet, guide pamphlets available at 50p each.

Disabled Access: Limited access, some parts of the garden are accessible to wheelchairs. The garden is a series of terraces, so involves flights of gentle steps.

Additional Information: Picnics allowed in front of the orangery and dogs must be kept on a leash.

HIDCOTE MANOR GARDEN

Chipping Campden, Glos., GL55 6LR.
(0386) 438333

Ownership: The National Trust.

Status: The National Trust.

General Description: One of the most famous of modern gardens, laid out by Major Lawrence Johnston over forty years, starting in 1907. The many formal and informal gardens are grouped together like a series of rooms, enclosed by superb hedges, and contain many rare trees, shrubs and plants of all kinds.

Open: April to end October, daily, except Tuesdays and Fridays, 11 a.m. – 7 p.m., no entry after 6 p.m. or one hour before sunset.

Admission: Adults: £4.20; Children: £2.10; Family: £11.60.

Facilities: Licensed restaurant serves morning coffee, lunches and teas.

Disabled Access: Part of garden only.

Additional Information: No dogs, picnics in car parks only.

HIGH BEECHES GARDENS

The High Beeches, Handcross, West Sussex, RH17 6HQ.
(0444) 400589

Ownership: High Beeches Gardens Conservation Trust.

Status: Historical Houses Association.

General Description: Twenty acres of enchanting woodland valley gardens, planted with magnolias, camellias, rhododendrons and azaleas, for spring. In autumn superbly landscaped with maples, liquidambers, amelanchiers and nyssas. Gentians, primulas, and iris are naturalised, with royal fern and gunnera in the Water Gardens. There are four acres of Wildflower Meadows, with cowslips and many orchids. The gardens are now declared 'Outstanding Historically' by English Heritage, and have been managed for the last twenty-five years by Anne and Edward Boscawen, who have accompanied botanical expeditions to the Himalayas, and other parts of the world.

Open: 20th April to 27th June and 5th September to 31st October, daily except Sunday and Wednesday, 1 p.m. – 5 p.m.

Admission: £2, accompanied children free.

Facilities: Ample car and coach parking, picnic area, barn tearoom, toilets, *refreshments on special event days only.*

Disabled Access: Tearoom, car park, toilets, special events.

Additional Information: Picnics, no dogs, conducted tours for groups by appointment, coaches by appointment.

THE SIR HAROLD HILLIER GARDENS AND ARBORETUM

Jermyns Lane, Ampfield, near Romsey, Hampshire, SO5 1OQA.
(0794) 68787

Ownership: Held in trust by Hampshire County Council.

General Description: In the heart of the Hampshire
countryside lies a plantsman's paradise, a garden for all
seasons, where there are plants of beauty and interest to be
enjoyed in every season of the year. These beautiful gardens
of 160 acres contain the largest collection of hardy trees and
shrubs of its kind in the British Isles and are filled with rare
and lovely plants. The collection was started by Sir Harold
Hillier, of the famous nursery family, in 1953 in the grounds
of his family home. With some 36,000 plants of 10,000
different species originating from all five continents, there is
something to delight in every season of the year, with
spectacular colour in spring and autumn. The massed
flamboyant blossoms of magnolias, rhododendrons and
azaleas in spring are followed by scented flowering shrubs in
summer. Autumn is a kaleidoscope of both vibrant and subtle
hues, as leaves turn colour and berries ripen, while the
strange spidery flowers of the witch hazels brighten dull
midwinter.

Open: Monday to Friday all year round, 10.30 a.m. – 5 p.m.
Weekends and Bank Holidays March to November 10.30
a.m. – 6 p.m.

Admission: Adult: £2.; Senior Citizens: £1.50; Child: 75p.

Facilities: Free and ample car parking, toilets, meals available at most times in the tearooms, trail leaflets and current interest sheets free at entrance.

Disabled Access: Disabled toilets, ramp to tearooms, wheelchair access to most areas of garden on gravel paths or grass paths, access to pond difficult, due to steep slope.

Additional Information: Picnic area with tables near entrance, no dogs.

HOLDENBY HOUSE AND GARDENS

Holdenby, Northants, NN6 8DJ.
(0604) 770074

Ownership: Mr. James Lowther.

Status: Historic Houses Association.

General Description: Once the largest house in Elizabethan England, Holdenby secured its place in history when it became the prison of Charles I during the Civil War. Today, Holdenby's falconry centre, collection of rare breeds of farm animals, children's cuddle farm, development of a seventeenth-century farmstead, craft shop, souvenir and plant shop, small museum, complement the beauty and history of the grounds with their Elizabethan and fragrant borders.

Open: April to end September, Sunday and Bank Holiday Mondays 2 p.m. – 6 p.m. House by appointment throughout year.

Admission: Gardens only – Adults: £2.50; Child: £1.20; Senior Citizens: £1.70; House and Gardens – Adult: £3.50; Child: £1.20.

Facilities: Large hard standing parking, Victorian kitchen tearoom serving home made teas, light snacks available for pre-booked parties.

Disabled Access: Hard standing, close to attractions, most attractions accessible but pea gravel paths, toilet facilities.

Additional Information: Picnic area available, children's play area, no dogs allowed except guide dogs.

HODNET HALL GARDENS

Hodnet, Market Drayton, Shropshire.
(0630) 84 202

Ownership: Mr. and the Hon. Mrs. Heber-Percy.

Status: Private ownership.

General Description: Over sixty acres of brilliantly coloured flowers, magnificent forest trees, sweeping lawns and a chain of ornamental pools which run tranquilly along the cultivated garden valley to provide a natural habitat for waterfowl and other wildlife. The gardens are carefully planted to provide a show of colour throughout the seasons, and won the Christies Garden of the Year Award in 1986.

Open: 1st April to 30th September, Monday to Saturday 2 – 5 p.m. Sundays and Bank Holidays 12 noon – 5.30 p.m.

Admission: Adults: £2.25; Senior Citizens: £2; Children: £1; Special rates for parties of twenty-five plus. Season tickets.

Facilities: Car and coach parks free of charge within easy walking distance of the lower lakes, gardens, tearooms, gift shop and toilets.

Disabled Access: Disabled toilets and access ramps to the tearooms, level access to the gift shop, wheelchairs available for use during visits to the gardens.

Additional Information: Picnic area, dogs kept on leads, refreshments are available in the half-timbered tearooms, plants and vegetables for sale in the kitchen garden.

HOLKER HALL AND GARDENS

Cark-in-Cartmel, Grange-over-Sands, Cumbria, LA11 7PL.
(05395) 58328

Ownership: Lord and Lady Cavendish.

Status: Historic Houses Association.

General Description: Magnificent formal and woodland
gardens, covering twenty-five acres, encompassed by the
Deer Park and Wildflower Meadow. In recent years the
gardens have been much improved by Lord and Lady
Cavendish. Inventive planting, the many rare and beautiful
shrubs and plants, water features such as the limestone
cascade, together with woodland walks make a visit to
Holker a must. In her book *Dream Gardens* Vivian Russell
says 'This is a garden of fulfilled visions, the product of two
gardening enthusiasts having the resources, imagination,
energy and taste to take a good garden and make it a great
one'. Further improvements will culminate in the opening of a
new floral garden designed by Lady Salisbury in the Spring
of 1992.

Open: 1st April to 31st October everyday excluding
Saturdays, 10.30 a.m. – 6 p.m. Last admission to grounds
4.30 p.m.

Admission: Gardens plus Deer Park and Audio Exhibitions –
Adult: £2.55; Children over 6 years: £1.45; Family Ticket (2
adults and up to 4 children): £7; Hall and Motor Museum
extra.

Facilities: Hardstanding and grass parking, cafeteria, gift shop, adventure playground, toddlers play area, picnic areas, craft and countryside exhibition, patchwork and quilting shop and Victorian/Edwardian and Wartime Kitchen exhibition.

Disabled Access: Disabled toilet, ramps.

Additional Information: Picnic area, dogs allowed if kept on a leash.

HOLKHAM HALL

Wells-next-the-Sea, Norfolk, NR23 1AB.
(0328) 710227

Ownership: Viscount Coke.

Status: Historic Houses Association.

General Description: Holkham Hall is an eighteenth-century
Palladian Mansion built between 1734 and 1762 by Thomas
Coke, 1st Earl of Leicester and houses a magnificent Art
Collection with works by Rubens, Van Dyck, Claude,
Poussin, Gainsborough together with many pieces of original
furniture and a collection of Greek and Roman Statuary. The
House is set in a walled and landscaped park of almost 3,000
acres of which a third is woodland including large numbers
of Ilex Oaks first introduced to Holkham in the seventeenth
century. The park contains a lake and about 750 head of
fallow deer. The architects and landscape gardeners whose
influence can still be seen are Kent, Brown, Eames, Wyatt,
Sandys and Repton.

Open: Easter, May, Spring & Summer Bank Holiday,
Sunday/Monday 11.30 a.m. – 5 p.m. Also open daily (except
Friday/Saturday) from late May to end of September.

Admission: Park: Free; House: £2.70.

Facilities: Parking for coaches and cars, light refreshments.

Disabled Access: Toilets.

Additional Information: Picnic in vicinity of car park, dogs
permitted on leads.

HOWICK HALL GARDENS

Howick, near Alnwick, Northumberland, NE66 3LB.
(0665) 577 285

Ownership: Howick Trustees Ltd.

General Description: Situated half a mile from the sea,
Howick has been the home of the Grey family since the
fourteenth century. The gardens were developed around the
Georgian house by the 5th Earl Grey and his wife from 1921
in the manner of William Robinson, and from 1963 by their
eldest daughter, Lady Mary Howick. Spring bulbs in
profusion in April lead on in May and June to a full display in
the woodland garden of rhododendrons, magnolias, azaleas
supported by varied ground cover plantings of primroses,
meconopsis, primulas, including many tender species
normally associated with the west coast of Scotland. Terraces
in front of the house with herbaceous borders are planted to
take over in late June through July and August. Many rare
small trees and shrubs give good autumn colour against a
background of mature forest trees. The emphasis throughout
the season is on a pleasant informality.

Open: April to October daily 1 p.m. – 6 p.m.

Admission: Adult: £1; Senior Citizens and children: 50p.

Facilities: Parking.

Disabled Access: Limited access.

Additional Information: No provision for picnics. 1992:
Dogs on a lead only. 1993: No dogs allowed.

KEW ROYAL BOTANIC GARDENS

Kew, Richmond, Surrey ,TW9 3AB.
(081) 940 1171

Ownership: Run by Board of Trustees.

General Description: In the garden, each season brings with it a new dimension: in spring the glorious crocus carpet, followed, later by bluebells. Bedding displays and the rose garden bring a riot of colour in high summer. Autumn brings memorable ranges of colour as the trees and shrubs change hue and the grass garden comes to maturity. As winter closes in, many trees display fascinating bark formations and there is year round interest provided by the thousands of plants in the tropical glasshouses. Set in the tranquil and spacious grounds at the southern end of the gardens, the Temperate House displays a rich and dramatic collection of plants from the subtropical areas of the world. In contrast the world famous Palm House allows the visitor to experience, at first hand, the intense heat and humidity of the rainforests where palms and tropical flowering plants thrive. In the subterranean area of the Palm House a stunning array of marine algae and plants are home to vividly coloured and, in some cases, remarkably shaped fish. Within the hot and humid area of the Princess of Wales Conservatory the giant Amazonian waterlily (*Victorias amazonica*) grows in close proximity to the mangrove swamp, while a few steps away, cacti and other succulents flourish in desert conditions. Kew's major exhibition building, the Sir Joseph Banks Building, is close to the main gate. Here, innovative and stimulating displays explain the importance of plants – the basis of life on Earth.

Open: Every day except Christmas Day and New Years Day. Open at 9.30 a.m., closing times vary from 4 p.m. to 6.30 p.m. on weekdays and from 4 p.m. to 8 p.m. on Sundays and Bank Holidays depending on time of sunset.

Admission: Adults: £3; Senior Citizens, Students: £1.50; Children (5-15): £1; Under 5: Free; Wheelchair user and attendant: £3; Individual season ticket: £12; Family season (2 adults and 3 children): £23.

Facilities: Car park, three restaurants, two art galleries, audio/visual exhibition, five major glasshouses, 300 acre grounds.

Disabled Access: Access to all facilities except Marianne North Gallery.

Additional Information: No dogs (except guide dogs), wheelchairs available on loan, picnics allowed in gardens.

KILLERTON

Broadclyst, Exeter, Devon, EX5 3LE.
(0392) 881345

Ownership: The National Trust.

Status: The National Trust.

General Description: The hillside gardens were laid out by Veitch in the late eighteenth and early nineteenth century. Today it is one of the National Trust's most important gardens for its plant content as it was used as a trial ground by Veitchs for plants collected around the world by the firm's plant hunters. Its sheltered position and lime-free soil made it ideal for new discoveries and many of the trees and shrubs growing in the garden today were the first of their kind to be raised in this country. Special features include the bear's hut, a thatched summer house named after a family pet that lived in it, an ice house, rare plants and shrubs, herbaceous borders.

Open: Garden, daily throughout the year, 11 a.m. – 5.30 p.m. (daylight hours in winter).

Admission: Adult: £2.40; Children half price.

Facilities: Parking, restaurant, self service tearoom, shop, plant centre, produce shop, exhibition on garden's history, toilets.

Disabled Access: Motorised buggies, with drivers for disabled visitors' garden tour, wheelchair access, adapted toilets.

Additional Information: No dogs in the garden but they are allowed in the park, picnics welcome, sixteenth-century costume displays.

KNEBWORTH HOUSE GARDENS

Knebworth, near Stevenage, Hertfordshire.
(0438) 812661

Ownership: Lord and Lady Cobbold.

Status: Historic Houses Association.

General Description: There have been gardens at Knebworth since the 1600's. The present layout dates from Victorian and Edwardian times, with more recent additions and alterations. The elaborate formal gardens of the Victorian era were simplified at the beginning of the twentieth century by Sir Edwin Lutyens, the well-known Edwardian architect, who married into the Lytton family. A main feature of the gardens is undoubtedly the twin pollared Lime Avenues planted in 1910 leading to the Upper Lawns of rose beds and colourful herbaceous borders with their backdrop of tall yew hedges. As well as a brick-paved garden and Gold Garden, a grass maze and a pets' cemetery, there is a 'Wilderness' area which is now undergoing new developments including the renovation of the pond. A recent addition to the garden is the reconstructed brick pergola. The unique quincunx pattern Herb Garden was designed for Knebworth in 1907 by Gertrude Jekyll and contains a delightful mixture of many herbs.

Open: 12 noon – Last admission 4.30 p.m. on the following dates: 4th and 5th April, 11th to 27th April, 2nd to 4th May, 9th and 10th May, 16th and 17th May, 23rd May to 30th July (closed 27th June), 4th August to 6th September, except closed Mondays (not including Bank Holiday Mondays) and 27th June. Open 12th and 13th September, 19th and 20th September, 26th and 27th September, 3rd and 4th October.

Admission: Adults: £4; Children, Senior Citizens: £3.50.

Facilities: Ample parking (free) close to house and gardens, restaurant, gift shop.

Disabled Access: Access to and around gardens via gravel paths – therefore limited access.

Additional Information: Picnics not allowed in gardens but they are allowed within the 250 acre Country Park in which the House and Gardens are set, dogs are allowed in the park, if kept on leads at all times, but are not allowed in the gardens.`

KNIGHTSHAYES COURT

Bolham, Tiverton, Devon, EX16 7RQ.
(0884) 254665

Ownership: The National Trust.

Status: The National Trust.

General Description: One of the finest gardens in Devon, renowned for rare plants and trees. The present garden was largely created in the 1950's by Sir John and Lady Amory. Special features include a lily pond garden created from an old bowling green, a paved garden of grey, silver and pink set among castellated yew hedges, topiary fox and hounds, there is a thirty acre garden in the wood with rhododendrons, azaleas ericas, meconopsis, primulas and peonies and many rarer plants from around the world, and tree species such as magnolias, birch, southern beech and maple.

Open: 1st April to 1st November, 10.30 a.m. – 5.30 p.m. daily.

Admission: Adult: £2.60; Children: half price.

Facilities: Parking, restaurant, shop including plant sales, toilets.

Disabled Access: Wheelchair access to parts of the garden, wheelchair available, adapted toilets, special parking near garden.

Additional Information: No dogs allowed in the garden, picnic area, Victorian Gothic house with striking decorated interior also open.

LANHYDROCK

Bodmin, Cornwall PL30 5AD.
(0208) 73320

Ownership: The National Trust.

Status: The National Trust.

General Description: Thirty acres of gardens surround a
nineteenth-century granite house built to replace the original
seventeenth-century house largely destroyed by fire. Formal
gardens to the front of the house also date from nineteenth
century and feature geometrically-shaped beds of roses
interspersed with clipped yews. Terraces feature beds of
annuals edged by box. Also an unusual herbaceous circular
bed within a boundary of yew which has a flowering season
from April to October. Garden features the NCCPG National
Collection of crocosmias. Beyond the parapet of the walled
garden lies a more informal area on the steep slopes rising
above the house. This includes large Himalayan magnolias,
rhododendrons, camellias and a stream edged with primulas,
astilbes, arums, rodgersias and other water-loving plants.

Open: 1st April to 1st November daily except Mondays when
the house only is closed, but open Bank Holiday Mondays.
11 a.m. – 5.30 p.m. Closes 5 p.m. in October. Last admission
¹/₂ hour before.

Admission: House: £4.80; Grounds: £2.40.

Facilities: Shop, restaurant, toilets.

Disabled Access: Formal garden has some gravel paths and a
few steps, Wild Garden is on a slope so difficult for
wheelchair access.

LEONARDSLEE GARDENS

Lower Beeding, Horsham, West Sussex, RH13 6PP.
(0403) 891212

Ownership: Loder family.

Status: Private ownership.

General Description: Leonardslee Gardens were created by
Sir Edmund Loder from 1889. Other Loder gardens in Sussex
included The High Beeches (Sir Edmund's father) and
Wakehurst Place (Gerald Loder, Sir Edmund's younger
brother) but only Leonardslee has the benefit of such a
fantastic setting. The gardens are situated in a beautiful and
extensive valley of over 200 acres with six lakes and
waterfalls and are world famous for their fabulous springtime
display of rhododendrons and azaleas. Delightful views
across the valley make this a photographer's paradise. There
is a splendid Rock Garden which is a kaleidoscope of colour
in spring, and a temperate greenhouse. Wallabies (introduced
here 100 years ago) hop about in part of the garden, and deer
(fallow and sika) roam in the parks. An exhibition of bonsai
trees in a Japanese courtyard has proved of considerable
interest, and, new for 1992, an Alpine House has been
created.

Open: Mid April to 30th June, everyday, 10 a.m. – 6 p.m. 1st
July to 31st October, Monday to Friday, 2 p.m. – 6 p.m.,
Saturdays and Sundays, 10 a.m. – 6 p.m.

Admission: Varies with season: April, June and October –
Adult: £3; Child: £1. May – Adult: £3.50; Child: £2. May
Sundays and May Bank Holiday – Adult: £4; Child: £2. July,
August and September – Adult: £2.50; Child: £1.

Facilities: Ample free parking, licensed restaurant, cafeteria,
gift shop, plants for sale.

Additional Information: Visitors may picnic in the grounds,
no dogs in the gardens, situated three miles from Handcross
(via A279) at bottom of M23.

LEVENS HALL AND TOPIARY GARDEN

Kendal, Cumbria, LA8 0PN.
(05395) 60321

Ownership: C. H. Bagot Esq.

Status: Historic Houses Association.

General Description: Rich in historical interest the house
contains, among its many treasures, a fine collection of
Jacobean furniture, paintings by Rubens, Lely and Cuyp,
Cromwellian armour, portraits and miniatures. Cordova
leather panels cover the dining room walls, and the earliest
English patchwork (c. 1708) is on display in one of the
bedrooms. The famous topiary garden is unique in age and
appearance, designed and planted by Monsieur Guillaume
Beaumont, it is one of the few remaining gardens in England
with its original design and many of its original trees. There
are magnificent tall trees of yew and box, clipped into
fanciful shapes, vast beech hedges, colourful bedding and
herbaceous borders. The nostalgia of the steam age can be
recalled when 'Bertha' a Fowler's Showman's engine and
'Little Gem' half-sized traction engine are in steam on
Sundays and Bank Holiday Mondays. An indoor collection of
model table engines illustrating the development of steam
power from 1820 to 1920 run under steam from 2 p.m. –
5 p.m.

Open: Easter Sunday to 30th September, Sundays to
Thursdays, 11 a.m. – 5 p.m. (last admission 4.30 p.m.). Steam
Collection 2 p.m. – 5 p.m.

Admission: House and Gardens – Adults: £3.50; Children: £1.90. Gardens only – Adults: £2.20; Children: £1.10, reductions for groups and Senior Citizens.

Facilities: Gift shop, plants for sale, homemade light lunches and teas, play and picnic areas.

Disabled Access: Disabled toilets, access to gardens but not house.

Additional Information: No dogs admitted, play and picnic areas available.

LINGHOLM GARDENS

Portinscale, Keswick, Cumbria, CA12 5UA.
(07687) 72003

Ownership: The Viscount Rochdale.

General Description: Lingholm Gardens have been developed from earlier this century when the main collection of rhododendrons and azaleas were planted by the first Lord Rochdale. The formal garden near the house includes a small memorial garden, herbaceous borders with a fine collection of miniature rhododendrons, and lawns interspersed with beds of begonias and roses. Continuing into the woodland garden, the main collection of rhododendrons and azaleas produces a riot of colour from April to June. Specialities also include meconopsis, and primulas, woodland shrubs and magnificent trees are also of considerable interest. Other garden features include early spring daffodils, cherry blossom, and magnificent autumn colours. A large selection of plants are available for sale in the nursery and greenhouses.

Open: 1st April to 31st October daily, 10 a.m. – 5 p.m.

Admission: Adults: £2.20; Accompanied children: free; Group rate for twenty-five and over.

Facilities: Free car park, toilets, tearoom.

Disabled Access: Disabled toilet, wheelchair 'route', entrance ramps, parking near entrance.

Additional Information: Picnic tables, no dogs except guide dogs.

LUTON HOO

Luton, Bedfordshire, LU1 3TQ.
(0582) 22955

Ownership: Trustees of Luton Hoo Foundation.

General Description: Luton Hoo was begun in 1767 by
Robert Adam and was remodelled at the beginning of this
century by Mews and Davies, architects of the Ritz Hotels in
London and Paris. The formal garden with its large
herbaceous borders on the south side of the house was laid out
by Romayne Walker and leads to the peaceful rock garden.
On the lower terrace is the rose garden and the surrounding
landscape is by 'Capability' Brown. Luton Hoo is now the
home of the Wernher Collection, one of the most complete
private fine art collections in Europe, including paintings,
furniture, tapestries and object d'art. There is also a large
display of the work of Carl Fabergé, jeweller to the Russian
court.

Open: 14th April to 18th October. Closed Mondays (except
Bank Holiday). Park and Gardens 12 noon – 6 p.m. House
1.30 p.m. – 5.45 p.m.

Admission: Adults: £4.30; Senior Citizens: £3.70; Children:
£1.75. Special rates for parties. Additional costs for private
tours or guides.

Facilities: Unlimited parking for coaches and cars,
restaurant/tearoom, gift shop.

Disabled Access: Access into house, lift to upper floor, ramp
in restaurant, full toilet facilities, accessible wheelchairs.

Additional Information: No dogs, picnic area available.

LYME PARK

Disley, Stockport, SK12 2NX
(0663) 762023

Ownership: The National Trust.

Status: The National Trust.

General Description: The impressive house dates from
Elizabeth I and visitors are welcomed to the hall by the
Edwardian servants of Lord Newton, who will delight to show
them the many treasures of Lyme. The house is surrounded by
seventeen acres of beautiful Victorian gardens. The gardens
contain an orangery by Wyatt, which houses Lyme's famous
200 year old Camellia (this Camellia flowers in May). Other
features in the garden include a sunken Dutch garden, with
fountain, a reflection lake, the Vicary Gibb garden, and a
wilderness garden called Killtime. Lyme is one of the few
properties, which has a seasonal bedding programme.

Open: Park open all year, gardens open all year except
Christmas Day and Boxing Day from 11 a.m. – 4 p.m. Winter
time, 11 a.m. – 5 p.m. summer time.

Admission: Park and Gardens is £3 per car with all occupants.

Disabled Access: On request at park admission point,
permission can be given to park outside hall. Access for
wheelchairs to gardens is limited. Please telephone for full
information. Disabled toilets are available in park and
gardens, and free electric wheelchair is available for use by
visitors.

Additional Information: Dogs are allowed in the gardens on lead, picnic areas are designated within the park, many attractions including information centre, countryside centre, through servants' eyes visitor centre, cream teas at the hall, refreshment kiosk in the park, shop, pitch and putt, nature trails and many more.

MAPPERTON GARDENS

Beaminster, Dorset, DT8 3NR.
(0308) 862645

Ownership: Mr. and Mrs. John Montagu.

General Description: Valley gardens descending below Tudor manor house from 1540s modified 1660s. Modern Italian art fountain court with orangery, topiary and stone ornaments. Seventeenth-century fish ponds, summer house and grottoes. Shrub garden and arboretum blending with pasture and woodland. Magnificent walks and views.

Open: March to October, daily, 2 p.m. – 6 p.m..

Admission: Adults: £2.50; Under 18: £1.50; Under 5's free.

Facilities: Parking close to attraction, house tours in groups of eighteen by appointment only, prices as for gardens, group rate for house tours £4.

Disabled Access: Upper levels only.

Additional Information: No dogs.

MARWOOD HILL GARDENS

Marwood, Barnstaple, Devon, EX31 4EB.
(0271) 42528

Ownership: Dr. J. A. Smart.

General Description: Eighteen acre garden, three small lakes with waterside planting, large collection of trees and shrubs, alpine scree. Walled garden with plant sales.

Open: All the year dawn to dusk, plant sales area every day 11 a.m. – 1 p.m., 2 p.m. – 5 p.m.

Admission: Adult: £1; Children: 10p.

Facilities: Free parking, toilets, teas in church hall on Sundays or parties by arrangement.

Disabled Access: Limited.

Additional Information: Dogs on leads, no picnics.

MOTTISFONT ABBEY GARDEN

Mottisfont, Romsey, Hampshire, SO51 0LQ.
(0794) 40757

Ownership: The National Trust.

Status: National Trust.

General Description: Bounded by a tributary of the River Test, the garden of Mottisfont Abbey forms a sheltered and tranquil setting for the former twelfth-century Augustinian Priory (now a private house). Although the garden is largely eighteenth century in character, the latter-day influences of Sir Geoffrey Jellicoe and Norah Lindsay are evident in the pleached lime avenue to the north of the House, and the box-edged parterre to the south. Notable among the many fine specimen trees is the 'Mottisfont Plane', reputed to be the largest of its kind in the country, while the ancient spring, or 'Font', from which the place name is derived, rises close by. Within the two walled flower gardens is gathered the National Collection of Old Fashioned Shrub Roses. Designed and planted in the 1970's by Graham Stuart Thomas, these gardens are seen at their best during the month of June and early July.

Open: April to September, Sunday to Thursday, 2 p.m. – 6 p.m.

Admission: Adults: £2.30; Child: £1.15.

Facilities: Parking, shop (including rose sales), refreshments available locally.

Disabled Access: Special parking areas available (please inquire at main car park kiosk on arrival), wheelchairs available, toilet facilities, most areas of the garden accessible by wheelchair.

Additional Information: Dogs in car park area only, light picnics allowed in main gardens.

MUNCASTER CASTLE

Ravenglass, Cumbria, CA18 1RQ.
(0229) 717614/717203

Ownership: Mrs. P. Gordon-Duff-Pennington.

Status: Historic Houses Association.

General Description: Muncaster Castle has grown through
the ages from the original fourteenth-century pele tower to
produce the fine building that you can see today. In the
eighteenth century John, 1st Lord Muncaster, created the
terrace with its breathtaking views of Scafell and the
Lakeland Fells, and planted many hardwood trees which
provided shelter from the wind to allow the present owner's
grandfather to create the famous rhododendron gardens in the
1920s. He subscribed to the Ludlow and Sheriff and Kingdon
Ward plant collecting expeditions and carried out a vigorous
crossing programme producing many new hybrids. Most of
these plants are still thriving at Muncaster, where the
proximity of the Gulf Stream and the acid soil have given
them an ideal habitat. There is a fine collection of magnolias,
camellias and maples, as well as hydrangeas and a large
collection of unusual trees, particularly the various species of
nothofagus.

Open: Gardens and owl centre open daily all year, 11 a.m. –
5 p.m. Castle open Tuesday to Sunday and all Bank Holiday
Mondays 1 p.m. – 4 p.m., 29th March to 1st November. Open
other times by appointment.

Admission: Castle, Gardens and Owl Centre – Adult: £4.50; Child: £2.50; Family Ticket (2 & 2): £12.00; Gardens and Owl Centre only – Adults: £2.80; Family Ticket: £7.50; Child: £1.50.

Facilities: Free car parking, stable butter, garden centre, nature trail, 'Meet the Birds' daily at 2.30 p.m. World of Owls audio-visual exhibition open daily. Adventure playground, gift shop and owl centre shop, water fowl pond.

Disabled Access: Small disabled car park near to centre of the facilities, disabled toilet.

Additional Information: Picnic area, dogs welcome on a lead (not allowed in castle).

NEWBY HALL AND GARDENS

Ripon, North Yorkshire, HG4 5AE.
(0423) 322583

Ownership: Mr. and Mrs. Robin Compton.

Status: Privately owned.

General Description: Beautiful late-seventeenth-century house in the style of Sir Christopher Wren with interiors by Robert Adam in 1760's. Superb Adam sculpture gallery, Gobelins tapestry room and library. Much fine Chippendale furniture. Twenty-five acres of formal gardens surround the famous double herbaceous borders, many rare and beautiful plants including the national collection of the *Genus Cornus* (Dogwoods). Miniature railway, children's adventure gardens, picnic area, shop, plant stall and garden restaurant. Special events including historic vehicles rally, two craft fairs and a country fair interspersed throughout the season.

Open: April to end September, Tuesday to Sundays (plus Bank Holiday Mondays). Gardens and restaurant 11 a.m. – 5.30 p.m. House 12 p.m. – 5 p.m.

Admission: House and Gardens – Adult: £4.80; Children: £2.70. Gardens only – Adult: £2.70; Children: £2. Special rates for Disabled visitors, Senior Citizens, Groups.

Facilities: Free large car park for cars and coaches, licensed garden restaurant (self-serve) with room adjacent for pre-booked parties. Function Room for pre-booked meetings/exhibitions (no audio visual shows).

Disabled Access: Five wheelchairs on free loan, good access round ground floor of house, good wheelchair route around gardens, map provided, disabled toilet facility adjacent restaurant.

Additional Information: Picnic area for garden visitors, adjacent to car park, dogs only allowed in enclosure adjacent to picnic area.

NUNWELL HOUSE AND GARDENS

Brading, Isle of Wight, PO36 0JQ.
(0983) 407240

Ownership: Mrs. J. A. Aylmer.

Status: Historic Houses Association, English Heritage.

General Description: The gardens cover some six acres and are documented from Sir John O'Glander's diaries written in about 1640. But much recent design work has gone on. Features include several borders, rose garden, a small arboretum and lavender steps, splendid Solent views across parkland in which some famous Nunwell Oaks survived the 1987 gale. Tender plants do well. Lawns with fountains. The whole garden has a tranquil setting and is kept a peaceful place.

Open: Sunday in July to last Thursday in September, Sunday to Thursday inclusive.

Admission: Adult: £2.30; Senior Citizens: £1.80; Accompanied children: 60p includes house entrance.

Facilities: Parking, gift shop, light refreshments, garden history exhibition.

Disabled Access: There are a number of steps but assistance is usually available.

Additional Information: Picnic areas available, no dogs in garden and house.

NYMANS GARDEN

Handcross, near Haywards Heath, West Sussex, RH17 6EB.
(0444) 400321 or 400002

Ownership: National Trust.

Status: National Trust.

General Description: One of the great gardens of the Sussex
weald, rare and beautiful plants, shrubs and trees from all
over the world, azaleas, rhododendrons, eucryphias,
hydrangeas, magnolias, camellias and roses, walled garden,
hidden sunk garden, pinetum, laurel walk, romantic ruins.

Open: 1st April to end October daily except Monday and
Friday (but open Bank Holiday Monday and Good Friday)
11 a.m. – 7 p.m. or sunset if earlier, last admissions one hour
before closing.

Admission: £3 (parties £2.50), car park at entrance, space
limited so coaches must book.

Facilities: Shop and exhibition 12 p.m. – 6 p.m. on same
days as garden, sandwiches, cakes and teas in teahouse near
car park.

Disabled Access: Garden accessible, special wheelchair route
indicated, toilets.

Additional Information: Dogs in car park only, events –
please send S.A.E. or telephone for information.

OXBURGH HALL

Oxborough, King's Lynn, Norfolk, PE33 9PS.
(036 621) 258

Ownership: The National Trust.

Status: National Trust.

General Description: Oxburgh Hall is a moated house built
in 1482 by the by the Bedingfeld family. Visited by Henry
VII, main features include the massive Tudor gatehouse, a
sixteenth-century priest's hole and embroidery worked by
Mary Queen of Scots during her captivity in England. The
garden has a colourful French parterre, laid out in the middle
of the nineteenth century, beautiful herbaceous borders, and
orchard, a victorian wilderness garden and a charming
woodland walk.

Open: 28th March to 1st November, Saturday to Wednesday
inclusive 1.30 p.m. – 5.30 p.m. Garden 12 p.m. – 5.30 p.m.,
Bank Holiday Mondays 11 a.m. – 5.30 p.m.

Admission: Adult: £3.50; Child (under 17): £1.75.

Facilities: Free parking, restaurant, shop.

Disabled Access: House 200 yards from car park, access
around moat, access to four routes in house. Toilet (adapted)
in west wing.

Additional Information: Picnics in car park only, no dogs
except guide dogs.

PACKWOOD HOUSE

Lapworth, Solihull, Warwickshire, B94 6AT.
(0564) 782024

Ownership: The National Trust.

Status: The National Trust.

General Description: Packwood lies in the pleasantly wooded Forest of Arden. For many years, it was the home of the Fetherstons, who allowed Cromwell's General, Henry Ireton, to sleep in the house before the Battle of Edgehill in 1642, but there is also a tradition that Charles II was given refreshment at Packwood after his defeat at Worcester in 1651. In 1905 it was bought by Mr. Alfred Ash, who together with his son, Graham Baron Ash, repaired the house and reinstated the seventeenth-century garden layout. A connoisseur's collection of furniture, tapestries and needlework is shown. If the famous seventeenth-century yew garden was laid out with the concept of the 'Sermon on the Mount' in mind or not is not known for certain.

Open: April to end of September, Wednesday to Sunday and Bank Holiday Monday 2 p.m. – 6 p.m. (Closed Good Friday). October – Wednesday to Sunday 12.30 p.m. – 4.30 p.m. Last admissions $^1/_2$ hr before closing.

Admission: House and Garden – Adults: £2.80; Children: £1.40. Garden only – Adult: £1.90; Family Ticket: £7.70.

Facilities: Free parking.

Disabled Access: Ground floor, toilets, wheelchair available.

Additional Information: Picnics.

PAINSWICK ROCOCO GARDENS

Painswick, Gloucestershire, GL6 6TH.
(0452) 813204

Status: Historic Houses Association.

General Description: The garden is currently being restored back to its original form as created in the 1740s. The restoration is based on a painting dated 1748 by Thomas Robins, work began in 1984 when the garden was in a complete state of abandonment. The garden dates from the brief Rococo period (1720-60) when the use of more natural elements and style were beginning to take over from strict formality. Emphasis was placed on walks and vistas incorporating buildings of varying architectural styles rather than a formal planting of flowers. The property (Painswick House) and gardens have always been in the same family. The current owner Lord Dickinson can trace his ancestry back to Charles Hyett who built the house in 1730. The garden is now leased to a charitable trust who manage it.

Open: 1st February to mid December, Wednesdays to Sundays 11 a.m. – 5 p.m.

Admission: Adult: £2.40; Senior Citizens: £2; Child: £1.20.

Facilities: Free parking, licensed restaurant for coffee, lunches and teas, gift shop.

Disabled Access: Access to toilets, restaurant, shop, but only to parts of the gardens.

Additional Information: Dogs allowed on leads, picnics.

PENCARROW HOUSE AND GARDENS

Washaway, Bodmin, Cornwall, PL30 3AG.
(020) 884 369

Ownership: The Molesworth-St. Aubyn Family.

Status: Historic Houses Association.

General Description: The garden is Grade II listed. It was
laid out by Sir William Molesworth Bt, PC, MP, the radical
statesman, starting in 1831. The Georgian house is
approached by a mile long drive, through an Ancient British
Encampment, flanked by huge rhododendrons, blue
hydrangeas and many specimen conifers which were
purchased in 1842. There is a formal Italian garden, a great
granite rockery, marked walks to the American gardens, Lake
and Ice House – fifty acres in all. In the early 1970s the
present owner started to clear the gardens, which had become
derelict during the war. By 1991 he had planted out more
than 160 different species of specimen conifers from all over
the world and planted more than 570 different species of
hybrids of the genus rhododendron, over sixty different
canellias as well as many broadleaved trees and flowering
shrubs often too tender to be grown outdoors except in the far
west.

Open: House, tearooms and craft centre open daily except
Friday and Saturday. Easter –15th October 1.30 p.m. – 5 p.m.
1st June to 10th September and Bank Holidays Mondays
11 a.m. Garden open daily during the season.

Admission: Gardens only: £1.50. House and gardens: £3.

Facilities: Ample parking in the stable yard. Tearooms – light lunches and cream teas. Craft centre, small children's play area. Plant shop, self pick soft fruit.

Disabled Access: Good access and toilet facilities.

Additional Information: Picnic area, dogs welcome off the lead when away from the formal gardens.

PENSHURST PLACE

Tonbridge, Kent, TN11 8DG.
(0892) 870307

Ownership: Privately owned by the 2nd Viscount De L'Isle.

General Description: The gardens at Penshurst Place are some of the most impressive formal gardens as well as oldest gardens in private ownership in Britain, planned at the same time as the house – six hundred years ago. The Tudor terraces are surrounded by a mile of clipped yew hedges; each of the twelve enclosures provide a contrast to its neighbour and a succession of colourful displays from spring to early autumn. The beautiful Kent countryside provides a magnificent setting for Penshurst Place, Gardens and Home Park with its Nature and Farm Trails. An arboretum was planted in early 1992 in memory of the first Viscount De L'Isle who spent many years restoring the gardens to their former glory. The gardens season ticket is new for 1992.

Open: 1st April to 4th October 1992, seven days a week. House and Grounds – 1 p.m. – 5.30 p.m. (last entry 5 p.m.). Grounds only – 11 a.m. – 6 p.m. (last entry 5 p.m.)

Admission: House and Grounds – Adult: £4; Child: £2.25; Senior Citizens, Students: £3.50. Grounds only – Adult: £3; Child: £2; Senor Citizens, Students: £2.50. Adult Group: £3.50 (min. of twenty people). Wheelchair visitors free. Gardens Season Ticket: £10 (includes Grounds and Venture Playground).

Facilities: Two car parks, capacity 450 cars, 20 coaches, restaurant, gift shop, museum and venture playground, nature and farm trails.

Disabled Access: Access to gardens, but limited to house due to age of buildings.

Additional Information: Guided tours available by arrangement, no dogs, school visits welcome, discounts negotiable.

POLESDEN LACEY

Great Bookham, Near Dorking, Surrey, RH5 6BD.
(0372) 458203 or 452048

Ownership: The National Trust.

Status: The National Trust.

General Description: Originally an 1820s Regency villa, remodelled after 1906 by the Hon. Mrs. Ronald Greville, well-known Edwardian hostess. Houses fine paintings, furniture, porcelain and silver, photographs from Mrs. Greville's albums. Extensive grounds, walled rose garden, lawns, views, King George VI and Queen Elizabeth (now the Queen Mother) spent part of their honeymoon here.

Open: House – March and November Saturday and Sunday only 1.30 p.m. – 4.30 p.m., 1st April to end October Wednesday to Sunday (inclusive Good Friday), 1.30 p.m. – 5.30 p.m., also open Bank Holiday Mondays and preceding Sundays 11 a.m. – 5.30 p.m. Grounds – daily all year, 11 a.m. – 6 p.m. Last admissions to house $^1/_2$ hr before closing.

Admission: Garden only – 1st April to end October: £2; November to end-March 1993: £1.50; House – Sunday and Bank Holiday Monday: £3.20 extra; other open days £2.50 extra. Parties: £4 (House and Garden) weekdays only by prior arrangement with Administrator.

Facilities: Shop. Coffee, lunches and home-made teas in licensed restaurant. Snack bar serving light refreshments at peak times. Picnic site by main car park.

Disabled Access: All showrooms and parts of garden, some fairly firm gravel paths. Disabled drivers may park near shop, restaurant and house with permission of Administrator. Toilet near restaurant.

Additional Information: Picnic site by main car park. No dogs in formal gardens, on paths or on lawns, allowed in rest of grounds on leads. Good walks on estate. No prams or pushchairs in house. Parking 150 yards.

RIPLEY CASTLE GARDENS

Ripley, Harrogate, North Yorkshire, HG3 3AY.
(0423) 770152

Ownership: Sir Thomas C. W. Ingilby B.G.

Status: Private ownership.

General Description: The walled gardens at Ripley Castle underwent an exciting transformation during 1991. The arrival of the National Historical Centre Collection created tremendous interest, and this has been enhance by the planting of 35,000 Dutch spring flowering bulbs in the gardens and grounds. The most radical development has been the upgrading of the orangery and hothouses to accommodate the fabulous tropical plant collection, transferred from Hull Botanical Gardens during 1991, and open to the public on a regular basis for the first time in 1992. Improvements in other parts of the walled gardens continue apace and the beautiful views over the lakes and deer park provide a wonderful setting.

Open: Daily April to October 11 a.m. – 5 p.m.

Admission: Adults: £2; Senior Citizens: £1.50; Children (under 16): £1.

Facilities: Ample free parking, castle open to the public, tearoom, shops, four star hotel accommodation, small playground for children.

Disabled Access: Good disabled access, disabled toilet at the local hotel (200 yards).

Additional Information: Dogs not allowed except guide dogs.

ROSEMOOR GARDEN

Great Torrington, Devon, EX38 8PH.
(0805) 24067

Status: Royal Horticultural Society.

General Description: The original garden, with species drawn world-wide, remains the jewel in Rosemoor's crown, but the fields are fast becoming a unique garden showpiece. Already well established are two formal rose gardens with 2,000 roses in 200 varieties, two colour theme gardens containing 7,000 plants in 700 varieties and herbaceous borders that will, one day, form a quarter mile ribbon of colour. This spring will see completion of the planting round the reservoir, which includes a stream and bog garden, the creation of a herb garden for disabled visitors to enjoy and a *potager* (ornamental kitchen garden). A visit to Rosemoor gives you the opportunity to buy and rare plants, and witness a new national garden in the making.

Open: Garden open all year, visitors centre 1st March to 31st October, April to September 10 a.m. – 6 p.m., March and October 10 a.m. – 5 p.m.

Admission: Adults: £2.25; Children: 50p; Parties of twenty and over £1.75 each. R.H.S. members free entry with guest.

Facilities: Free car park, shop and plant sales area, licensed restaurant, coaches welcome by appointment.

Disabled Access: Full facilities for disabled visitors, wheelchairs available upon request.

Additional Information: Picnic area, guide dogs only.

ROUSHAM HOUSE AND GARDENS

Near Steeple Aston, Oxon, OX5 3QX.
(0869) 47110

Status: Private.

General Description: Rousham and its landscape garden should be a place of pilgrimage for students of the work of William Kent (1685-1748). Rousham represents the first phase of English landscape design and remains almost as Kent left it. The house, built in 1635 by Sir Robert Dormer, is still in the ownership of the same family. Kent added wings and the stable block, and made alterations to the interior of the house, which retains some seventeenth-century panelling, and the original staircases, furniture, pictures and bronzes. Don't miss the walled garden with herbaceous borders, parterre, pigeon house and espalier apple trees. A fine herd of rare long-horn cattle are to be seen in the park. Rousham is uncommercial and unspoilt with no tearoom and no shop. Bring a picnic, wear comfortable shoes and it is yours for the day.

Open: House, April to September inclusive, Wednesday, Sundays and Bank Holidays 2 p.m. – 4.30 p.m. Garden, daily all year 10.30 a.m. – 4.30 p.m.

Admission: House: £2; Garden: £2.

Facilities: Free parking.

Disabled Access: Limited access to garden only.

Additional Information: Picnics welcome in garden, no dogs or children under fifteen.

SAVILL GARDEN

Wick Lane, Englefield Green, Egham, Surrey.
(0753) 860222

Ownership: Crown Estate Commissioners.

General Description: A world renowned woodland garden of thirty-five acres providing a wealth of beauty and interest at all seasons. Spring is heralded by hosts of daffodils, masses of rhododendrons, azaleas, camellias, magnolias and much more. Suitable herbaceous plants for moist woodland conditions also feature and here such plants as primulas, meconopsis, hostas and ferns flourish. The hundreds of roses, herbaceous borders and countless alpines are the great feature of summer, and the leaf colours and fruits of autumn rival the other seasons with a great display. Winter has also much to offer and is by no means a dull period. Truly a garden for all seasons.

Open: Daily (closed 25th to 28th December). 10 a.m. – 6 p.m. (7 p.m. at weekends) or sunset when earlier.

Admission: Adults: £2.50; Senior Citizens: £2.30; Parties of twenty or more: £2.30. Accompanied children under sixteen free (limited to three per adult).

Facilities: Free car/coach parking, self-service restaurant, gift shop and plant centre.

Disabled Access: Wheelchair access and disabled toilets.

Additional Information: No dogs or picnics allowed in the garden. There is a picnic area adjacent to the car/coach park.

SCOTNEY CASTLE GARDEN

Lamberhurst, Kent ,TN3 8JN.
(0892) 890651

Ownership: National Trust.

Status: National Trust.

General Description: A famous picturesque landscape garden, surrounding the moated ruins of a fourteenth-century castle. The garden was created by the Hussey family in the 1840s and in 1970 Mr. Christopher Hussey bequeathed most of his estate to the National Trust. The garden slopes steeply, down to the romantic ruins of the Old Castle, with many rare plants and colour all year round. In late winter there are snowdrops, followed by daffodils. Magnolia and Japanese maples in spring, followed by rhododendrons in May and June. Autumn brings wonderful colour from the delicately balanced deciduous and evergreen trees and shrubs. On the slope of the garden there is an ice-house, a tent-shape structure thatched with heather. Ice cut from the moat in winter was stored there for use in summer, before the days of refrigerators.

Open: April to 8th November, Wednesday to Friday, 11 a.m. – 6 p.m. (or sunset if earlier), Saturday, Sunday and Bank Holiday Monday, 2 p.m. – 6 p.m. (or sunset if earlier), closed Good Friday.

Admission: Wednesday to Saturday – Adults: £2.40; Children: £1.20; Sunday and Bank Holiday Monday – Adults: £3; Children: £1.50.

Facilities: Car parking, shop open as property plus Christmas.

Disabled Access: Partly accessible to wheelchair users, but strong companion necessary, path very steep in places.

Additional Information: Picnics allowed on grass area near car park, no dogs in garden.

SHEFFIELD PARK GARDEN

Near Uckfield, East Sussex.
(0825) 790231

Ownership: The National Trust.

Status: The National Trust.

General Description: A very fine eighteenth-century garden with five lakes a very large collection of trees and shrubs. Rhododendrons and azaleas in May, water lilies in summer, and wonderful autumn colours, also bluebells and daffodils. Part of the garden was laid out by 'Capability' Brown and by Repton.

Open: April to 8th November, Tuesday to Saturday 11 a.m. – 6 p.m. (or sunset if earlier). Sunday and Bank Holiday Monday, 2 p.m. – 6 p.m. (or sunset if earlier). Last admission 1 hr. before closing. Sundays in October and November 1 p.m. to sunset. Closed Good Friday.

Admission: May, October, November – Adult: £3.70; Children: £1.90; parties of fifteen or more: £2.60; Children: £1.30. April and June to end September – Adult: £3.20; Children: £1.60; parties of fifteen or more: £2.10; Children: £1.10. No reduction for parties on Saturday, Sunday or Bank Holiday Monday.

Disabled Access: Disabled route and toilets.

Additional Information: Dogs not allowed, picnic area adjacent to car park, car and coach parking free.

SHERINGHAM PARK

Sheringham, Norfolk, NR26 8TB.
(0263) 823778

Ownership: National Trust.

Status: National Trust.

General Description: Historic landscaped park designed by, and the greatest work of, Humphrey Repton. Classic seascape views from park, broadwalk and gazebos, fifty-acre wild garden with important collection of azaleas and rhododendrons among others. Waymarked walks through mature woodland, parkland to sea cliffs.

Open: Every day dawn till dusk except Christmas Eve (when closed all day).

Admission: £2.10 per car; £6 per coach.

Facilities: Car park, toilets, information guide, refreshment available at nearby Felbrigg Hall.

Disabled Access: Adapted toilets, boarded walkway, electric and manual wheelchair available, Easter – end October on first come first served basis.

Additional Information: Picnic tables/area, dogs admitted under strict control.

SHUGBOROUGH ESTATE

Milford, near Stafford, Staffordshire, ST17 0XB.
(0889) 881388

Ownership: Owned by National Trust, financed and administered by Staffordshire County Council.

Status: National Trust.

General Description: Shugborough is the magnificent 900 acre seat of the Earls of Lichfield. The eighteenth-century Mansion House contains fine collections of ceramics, silver, paintings and French furniture. Part of the house continues to be lived in by the 5th Earl, Royal photographer Patrick Lichfield. Visitors can enjoy the nineteen acre Grade One historic garden including rose garden and a unique collection of neo-classical monuments. Other attractions include Staffordshire County Museum housed in the original servants quarters. The laundry, kitchens, brewhouse and coachhouses have been lovingly restored showing how servants lived and worked 100 years ago. Shugborough Park Farm is a Georgian farmstead that features an agricultural museum, working water-driven corn mill and rare breeds centre. Traditional farming methods are used to demonstrate farmhouse cooking, butter and cheese making in the dairy, breadmaking, hand milking and shire horse work.

Open: Easter to October, daily 11 a.m. – 5 p.m. Open Bank Holidays.

Admission: £1 per car (parking fee) includes entrance to gardens and parkland. Mansion, museum and farm – Adults: £3 each site; Concessionary rate: £2 each site.

Facilities: Parking, tearooms, National Trust gift shop, school demonstration, adult party bookings, packages, events, exhibitions.

Disabled Access: Disabled access to mansion and museum and farm (ground floor only), disabled parking and toilets.

Additional Information: Picnic areas, dogs allowed on leads in gardens and parkland only.

SIZERGH CASTLE

Near Kendal, Cumbria, LA8 8AE.
(05395) 60070

Ownership: National Trust.

Status: National Trust.

General Description: The Strickland family home for more than 750 years, impressive fourteenth-century pele tower, extended in Tudor times, with some of the finest Elizabethan carved overmantels in the country, good English and French furniture and family portraits surrounded by gardens including the Trust's largest limestone rock garden, good autumn colour.

Open: 1st April to 29th October, Sunday to Thursday 1.30 p.m. – 5.30 p.m. Garden as Castle from 12.30 p.m. Last admissions 5 p.m.

Admission: Adult: £3.10; Child: £1.60; Parties of fifteen or more: £2.30 by arrangement with the Administrator (not Bank Holidays).

Facilities: Parking 100 yards from Castle, tearoom open 1.30 p.m. same days as Castle.

Disabled Access: Most of garden mainly via paths, Lower Hall and tea room accessible.

Additional Information: Picnic tables in car park.

SOMERLEYTON HALL AND GARDENS

Somerleyton Hall, Lowestoft, Suffolk, NR32 5QQ.
(0502) 730224. Fax: (0502) 732143

Ownership: The Rt. Hon. Lord Somerleyton D.L.

Status: Historic Houses Association.

General Description: The home of Lord and Lady
Somerleyton. The house, with its state room possesses fine
furniture and paintings. The twelve acres of gardens are
renowned. The yew hedge maze planted by Nesfield (1846)
is a rare and beautiful example of the Victorian maze. There
are colourful hybrid and species rhododendrons and azaleas
and a long pergola trailing wisteria set among fine evergreen
trees. Other notable features – sunken garden, loggia
tearoom, Paxton glasshouses, aviary, statuary, a Villiamy
chiming clock in the stable block.

Open: Easter Day to 27th September, Sundays, Bank
Holidays, Thursdays 2 p.m. – 5.30 p.m. July and August,
Sundays, Bank Holidays, Tuesday, Wednesday, Thursday,
2 p.m. – 5.30 p.m.

Admission: Adult: £3.40; Senior Citizens: £2.70; Child:
£1.65; Parties – Adult and Senior Citizens: £2.40; Children:
£1.35.

Facilities: Car/bus park, picnic area, loggia tearoom, shop.

Disabled Access: Comprehensive.

Additional Information: No dogs allowed.

SPETCHLEY PARK GARDEN

Spetchley Park, Worcester, WR5 1RS.
(090565) 213/224

Ownership: Mr. and Mrs. R. J. Berkeley.

Status: Historic Houses Association.

General Description: This large private garden, covering thirty acres, has been in the Berkeley family since 1605. At Spetchley you will find most aspects of gardening, formal and informal, woodland and herbaceous. A garden full of secrets, every corner reveals some new vista, some treasure of the plant world. April produces a wonderful display of daffodils and other bulbs. April and May are also the months of flowering trees and shrubs, many rare and unusual. The large collection of roses come into their own in June and July, whilst July, August and September reveal the herbaceous borders in all their glory.

Open: 1st April to 30th September, Tuesdays to Fridays 11 a.m. – 5 p.m. Sundays 2 p.m. – 5 p.m. Bank Holiday Mondays 11 a.m. – 5 p.m.

Admission: Adults: £1.80; Children: 90p; Reduced rates for pre-booked parties of twenty-five or more persons.

Facilities: Parking, tearoom, plant sales, toilets.

Disabled Access: Wheelchair access to most of garden.

Additional Information: No dogs in gardens, picnics allowed out of sight of house.

STOURHEAD GARDEN

Stourton, near Warminster, Wiltshire, BA12 6QH.
(0747) 840348

Ownership: The National Trust.

Status: The National Trust.

General Description: Magnificent landscape garden created by Henry Hoare II, the wealthy banker, from 1741-80 as a reaction against formal gardens of the seventeenth century. 'Natural' landscape dotted with classical eye catchers surrounds a long artificial lake and presents an English eighteenth-century view of an arcadian paradise. Follies include a Pantheon, Temple of Apollo, Temple of Flora and a dripping grotto with a silver god. Richard Colt Hoare, grandson of Henry, added to the garden by planting unusual trees and shrubs but left his grandfather's basic scheme unaltered. Daffodils carpet the grounds in spring when magnolias are in flower and a stunning display of rhododendrons follows in early summer. Japanese, Norwegian, broadleaf maples, tulip trees and other exotics give a blazing autumn display.

Open: All year round 8 a.m. – 7 p.m. or dusk if earlier except 22nd – 25th July when garden closes at 5 p.m.

Admission: 1st March to end October: £3.60; Child: £1.80; Party: £3.20. November to end February: £2.60; Child: £1.30. Separate times/prices apply for Stourhead House.

Facilities: Ample parking, shop, refreshments available (tearoom and inn).

Disabled Access: Route around lake accessible to wheelchair users, toilets in local inn.

Additional Information: Dogs only allowed in winter months, guide dogs allowed all year, November to end February on leads.

SUTTON PARK STATELY HOME

Sutton on the Forest, York, YO6 1DP.
(0347) 810249

Ownership: Mrs. N. M. D. Sheffield.

General Description: Sutton Park is a charming example of early Georgian architecture, the architect is thought to have been Thomas Atkinson. The house is full of wonderful furniture, porcelain, beadwork, needlepoint and paintings. In every room there are fresh flower arrangements with flowers picked from the garden. The garden lies to the south side of the House, overlooking parkland thought to have been designed by 'Capability' Brown. There are three terraces with a lily canal on the third terrace. The pathways are made of York stone and flowers have been allowed to seed in the crevices. There are borders full of scented plants, sweeping lawns, mature trees, walks through semi-wild glades smothered with narcissi and daffodils. Herbaceous and rose borders are filled with many rare plants and Mrs. Sheffield's enormous enthusiasm for her garden shows in her great care with which collections of plants have been selected.

Open: Gardens open daily from 11 a.m. until 5.30 p.m. Easter to October. House open every Wednesday 6th May to 9th September, all Easter weekend and every Bank Holiday Sunday and Monday, from 1.30 p.m. – 5.30 p.m. Private parties are welcome any day of the week except Saturday, by appointment only.

Admission: House and Gardens – Adults: £3; Children: £1.50; Senior Citizens and Coach Parties: £2.50. Gardens only – Adult: £1; Children: 50p; Senior Citizens and Coach Parties: £1.

Facilities: Tearoom, gift shop, free parking.

Disabled Access: Gardens only, wheelchairs with pushers gardens only.

Additional Information: Dogs allowed in gardens on leads.

SYON PARK

Syon Park, Brentford, Middlesex ,TW7 8JF.
(081) 560 0881

Ownership: The Duke of Northumberland.

Status: Historic Houses Association (privately owned).

General Description: Fifty-five acres of pleasure gardens and lake set in 'Capability' Brown park. Gardens contain one of England's oldest great conservatories – designed by Charles Fowler in 1820. Newly restored and planted for colour and scent garden adjacent to Syon House, London home of the Piercey family since fourteenth century. Public rooms are said to be Robert Adam's finest work.

Open: Gardens every day except Christmas Day and Boxing Day 10 a.m. – 6 p.m. (summer). 10 a.m. – Dusk (winter).

Admission: Adults: £1.50; Senior Citizens/Child: £1; Schools: 50p.

Facilities: Ample free parking, cafeteria and restaurant.

Disabled Access: Good access to gardens and conservatory.

Additional Information: No dogs, picnics anywhere.

TATTON PARK

Knutsford, Cheshire, WA16 6DN.
(0565) 654822. Infoline: (0565) 750250

Ownership: The National Trust.

Status: The National Trust.

General Description: Tatton's magnificent gardens are of national importance. The glasshouses, namely the fernery and orangery, are probably the finest of their kind in the National Trust. Many other features are notable, especially famous is the Japanese garden which was constructed by Japanese workers brought over at the turn of the century. The gardens are most popular during the display of azaleas and rhododendrons, some hybrid species of which are unique to Tatton. The Italian garden, Greek monument, redwoods and African hut lend a special international flavour to Tatton. The estate consists of a mansion, medieval hall, working 1930s farm and deer park with two lakes as well as the gardens. Covering fifty acres there are delightful surprises at every turn.

Open: Daily except Monday 10.30 a.m. – 6 p.m.

Admission: Adult: £2.30; Child (5-15): £1.60.

Disabled Access: Wheelchair access to the gardens.

Additional Information: Children's adventure playground, dogs are not allowed in the gardens.

TINTINHULL HOUSE GARDEN

Tintinhull, near Yeovil, Somerset, BA22 9PZ.

Ownership: The National Trust.

Status: The National Trust.

General Description: Twentieth-century formal garden surrounding a seventeenth-century house (not open to public). The layout, divided into areas by walls and hedges, has border colour and plant themes, shrub roses, clematis and kitchen garden.

Open: 1st April to 30th September, Wednesdays, Thursdays, Saturdays and Bank Holidays. Mondays 2 p.m. – 6 p.m.

Admission: £2.80; coach parties by prior arrangement.

Facilities: Refreshments available.

Disabled Access: Suitable for physically and visually disabled visitors.

Additional Information: No dogs.

THORP PERROW ARBORETUM

Bedale, North Yorkshire, DL8 2PR.
(0677) 425323

Ownership: Sir John Ropner B.T.

Status: Private ownership.

General Description: A magnificent collection of over 1,000 different trees and shrubs from around the world, some are the largest and or rarest of their type in Great Britain. The arboretum comprises approximately eighty-five acres with three main areas: a) Ancient Woodland (Spring Wood) that borders the lake; b) A Victorian Pinetum (Milbank Pinetum) planted 1840-1870; c) The main arboretum (approximately sixty-five acres), designed and planted by Sir Leonard Ropner from 1931-77. The whole area is aesthetically pleasing (as well as being of scientific value) with superb spring, summer and autumn display; and provides an excellent day out for enthusiasts and family alike. Features include a large lake, with access to Kate's Island and Henry's Island, woodland walks, grassy glades, tree trails and Milbank Pinetum. The arboretum houses four national collections: oak, ash, lime and walnuts.

Open: All year from dawn to dusk (every day of the year).

Admission: Adults: £2; Children, Senior Citizens, UB40: £1.

Facilities: Large car/coach park, toilets.

Disabled Access: Access for the disabled visitors generally good in fine weather, can be very slippery in wet.

Additional Information: Picnic area, dogs allowed on lead.

TREBAH GARDEN

Mawnam Smith, near Falmouth, Cornwall, TR11 5JZ.
(0326) 250448

Ownership: Trebah Garden Trust.

Status: English Heritage

General Description: 'Like a corner of the Himalayas only better cared for'. Trebah stands in an amphitheatre of large trees at the head of a 200 feet ravine running down to the Hertford River near Falmouth. First recorded in the Domesday Book the dramatic and uniquely beautiful garden was laid out in the 1840s by Charles Fox. The upper garden is planted as a dry Mediterranean terrace. The water gardens run down from the house to the private beach with waterfalls, a koi pool, several ponds with massed primulas and zantedeschia and through two acres of massed hydrangeas. The lower slopes are covered with a sub-tropical rain forest with 100 year old rhododendrons, magnolias, pieris, azaleas and camellias and glades of giant tree ferns and gunnera manicata. Special activities and interests are provided for children. This is a magical garden, full of colour throughout the year and a paradise for the plantsman, the artist and the family.

Open: Every day throughout the year, 10.30 a.m. – 5 p.m.

Admission: Adults: £2.50; Children (5-15) and Disabled: £1; Children under 5 free; Organised parties of twelve or more: £2 per person.

Facilities: Free parking for cars and coaches, garden shop with light refreshments, covered seating for sixty.

Disabled Access: Limited access and facilities for disabled visitors.

Additional Information: Visitors welcome to use private beach on mouth of Hertford River, and may bring picnics, dogs welcome on leads.

TRELISSICK GARDEN

Feock, Truro, Cornwall, TR3 6QL.
(0872) 862090

Ownership: The National Trust.

Status: The National Trust.

General Description: Four hundred acres of garden, park and farmland was given to the National Trust in 1955 by Mrs. Ida Copeland. The quality of the garden and magnificent setting of sweeping parkland and miles of woodland paths lapped by the waters of the Fal make Trelissick one of the most popular and beautiful estates in Cornwall. The house, built originally in 1750 but considerably enlarged in the nineteenth century, is occupied privately and is not open to the public. The woodland garden, with its hidden corners and summer houses, is perhaps at its best in springtime when the collection of camellias, magnolias and rhododendrons are in flower, but the variety of tender and exotic trees and shrubs ensures all year round beauty and interest. The open parkland enjoys superb views down the broad expanse of Carrick Roads to Pendennis Castle and the sea. Around the edge of the estate there is a woodland walk through oak and beechwoods beside the water.

Open: 1st March to 31st October, 10.30 a.m. – 5.30 p.m. except Sundays 1 p.m. – 5.30 p.m. Closes 5 p.m. in March and October.

Admission: £2.80 (Children half price).

Facilities: Parking, art and craft gallery, shop, plant sales, restaurant, open air events, theatre in summer.

Disabled Access: Main part of the garden is flat and accessible to wheel chairs, toilet.

Additional Information: Parkland and woodland walk with wide river views open at all times, dogs not permitted in garden but may be exercised in park and woodland (under control).

TRENGWAINTON GARDEN

Near Penzance, Cornwall, TR20 8RZ.
(0736) 63021

Ownership: The National Trust.

Status: National Trust.

General Description: The most tender and exotic shrubs flourish in the mild maritime climate of Trengwainton and are further protected by a unique system of five walled gardens. It is particularly beautiful in Spring and early Summer, when there are impressive displays of magnolias, rhododendrons and azaleas. The present garden was largely created by Lt. Col. Sir Edward Bolitho. He recognised the talents of the Head Gardener, A. Creek, as a propagator, and allowed him full scope to use them. The magnificent rhododendron collection was largely raised from seed brought back from Kingdon-Ward's plant hunting expedition to India and Burma in the late 1920s. Sir Edward gave Trengwainton to the National Trust in 1961, and the family still live in the house (which is not open to the public).

Open: 1st March to 30th October, Wednesday to Saturday and Bank Holiday Mondays, 10.30 a.m. – 5.30 p.m. (5 p.m. in March and October). Last admission half hour before closing.

Admission: £2.20.

Facilities: Parking, small selection of plants, teas usually available at nearby Trengwainton Farm, toilets.

Disabled Access: Disabled access to some parts of garden, braille guide.

Additional Information: No dogs except guide dogs.

TRERICE

Near Newquay, Cornwall, TR8 4PG.
(0637) 875404

Status: The National Trust.

General Description: Small summer garden with enclosed
courts, lawns and bowling green. Garden surrounds
Elizabethan house but no surviving or reconstructed features
from that period. Orchard of fruit trees planted in seventeenth
century quincunx pattern. Collection of perennials, climbers
and shrubs. Back court with fuchsias, lonicera and roses.
Front walled courtyard with herbaceous borders.
Extraordinary collection of lawnmowers in hayloft of former
stable.

Open: 1st April to 1st November, daily except Tuesdays,
11 a.m. – 5 p.m., closes 5 p.m., in Ocober. Last admission
half hour before closing.

Admission: £3.40; Party bookings: £2.80.

Facilities: Refreshments, shop, toilets.

Disabled Access: Garden not easily accessible by wheelchair,
toilets for disabled.

UPTON HOUSE

Banbury , Oxfordshire, OX15 6HT.
(0295 87) 266

Ownership: The National Trust.

Status: The National Trust.

General Description: Late seventeenth-century house remodelled 1927-29 for the Second Viscount Bearsted. The outstanding collection of paintings includes works by El Greco, Brueghel, Bosch, Memling, Guardi, Hogarth and Stubbs. Brussels tapestries, Sèvres porcelain, Chelsea figures. Large garden with wide lawns and terraced herbaceous borders which descend to lakes and the bog garden in a deep valley.

Open: April and October, Saturday, Sunday and Bank Holiday Mondays, 2 p.m. – 6 p.m. May to September, Saturday to Wednesday including Bank Holiday Mondays 2 p.m. – 6 p.m. Last admissions to house 5.30 p.m.

Admission: Adults: £3.50; Children: £1.75; Family ticket: £9.60; Garden only: £2.

Facilities: Free car parking, tearoom open as house.

Disabled Access: Disabled toilets, access ground floor only, motorised buggy with drivers available for access to/from lower garden.

Additional Information: No dogs.

WADDESDON MANOR

Waddesdon, Aylesbury, Bucks., HP18 0JH.
(0296) 651211

Ownership: The National Trust.

Status: The National Trust.

General Description: In 1874 Baron Ferdinand de Rothschild acquired the Buckinghamshire hilltop which became the site for the Destailleur designed château, around which is set one of the finest late Victorian formal gardens and parks designed by Lainé. The elegant cast iron rococco style aviary, built in 1889, contains mainly softbill birds and some parrots. House closed for refurbishment during 1992. Open again in 1993. Grounds, aviary, gift shop and tearoom remain open during 1992.

Open: The grounds and aviary, restaurant and shops are open from 12 a.m. – 5 p.m., Wednesday to Friday (inclusive) and from 12 noon – 6 p.m. at weekends, Good Friday, and Bank Holiday Mondays from 18th March to 23rd December 1992.

Admission: Grounds and Aviary – Adults: £3; Children 5-17 years: £1.50; Children under 5's years free.

Facilities: Parking and entry to the restaurant and shops free.

Disabled Access: Gift shop and tearoom easily accessible, most of garden and grounds easy, some gravel, toilets.

Additional Information: Picnics welcome, dogs not admitted except guide dogs.

WALLINGTON

Cambo, Morpeth, Northumbria, NE61 4AR.
(Scots Gap) 283

Ownership: The National Trust.

Status: The National Trust.

General Description: The Walled Garden – This garden at
the lower end of the East Wood is full of interest and beauty
with fine terraces, an outstanding collection of trees and
shrubs and a great variety of herbaceous, alpine and bulbous
plants. The entrance is through the Neptune Gate, which
takes its name from the surmounting statue. This and the row
of early eighteenth-century lead figures on the conservatory
terrace may originally have come from Blacketts' house in
Newcastle. Below the terrace is the pool and water garden
designed by Mary, Lady Trevelyan in 1938. Behind are the
conservatories with their magnificent fuchsias, and the Owl
House built in about 1765 when the Walled Garden was first
created as a kitchen garden. At the far eastern end of the
conservatory terrace there is a splendid view of James Paine's
Bridge built over the Wansbeck in 1755.

Open: House – 1st April to 31st October daily, 1 p.m. –
5.30 p.m. (closed Tuesdays). Last admission 5 p.m. Grounds
– open all year during daylight hours. Walled Garden –
Easter to September, 10.30 a.m. – 7 p.m., October to March,
10.30 a.m. – 4.30 p.m. Clock Tower Restaurant, Information
Centre and Shop 1st April to 31st October 10.30 a.m. – 5.30
p.m. (closed Thursdays), November to December,
Wednesday to Sunday 12.30 p.m. – 4.30 p.m.

Admission: House, garden and grounds: £3.80; Children up to 17: half price. Ground only: £1.80; Children: half price.

Facilities: Parking for coaches and cars, toilets.

Disabled Access: Car parking for disabled visitors is available in the car park and at the Walled Garden on application to the car park attendant. A wheelchair is available to take less able visitors from the car park to the house and also to the Walled Garden, toilets.

Additional Information: Picnics are allowed anywhere *except* the Walled Garden, dogs on leads in Walled Garden.

WESTONBIRT ARBORETUM

Forestry Commission, Westonbirt Arboretum, Tetbury, Glos.
GL8 8QS.
(0666) 88 220

Ownership: Forestry Commission.

General Description: Westonbirt Arboretum was started in
1829 by Robert Halford and extended by his son Sir George.
In 1956 the Forestry Commission took over the management
and opened the arboretum to the public. Westonbirt
Arboretum is today one of the finest tree and shrub
collections in Europe. With 18,000 numbered trees and
shrubs it is a joy to visit at anytime of year, but especially in
the spring and autumn. Enjoy a tranquil walk amongst the
many wild flowers, birds, butterflies and fungi that thrive in
the 600 acres of landscaped grounds.

Open: Grounds every day of the year, visitor centre and open
air: cafe Easter to mid-November.

Admission: Adult: £2; Senior Citizens: £1.50; Child: £1.

Facilities: Visitor centre, exhibition, audio/visual
presentation, gift shop, open air cafe, trails/walks, toilets, car
park.

Disabled Access: Toilet, access to visitor centre and cafe
good, paths level but a little uneven.

Additional Information: Dogs allowed on most of area,
picnic areas.

WILTON HOUSE

Near Salisbury, Wiltshire, SP2 0BJ.
(0722) 743115

Ownership: The Earl of Pembroke.

Status: Privately owned.

General Description: Wilton House has been the home of the Earls of Pembroke for over 400 years. The grounds are Parkland setting with an arboretum, herbaceous borders, rose and Japanese water garden. A fine feature of the grounds is the Palladian Bridge which spans the river Nadder.

Open: 7th April to 18th October 1992 Mondays to Saturdays inclusive 11 a.m. – 6 p.m. Sundays noon – 6 p.m. Last admission 4.45 p.m.

Admission: Grounds only – Adults: £2; Children over 5 and under 16 years: £1.50. To the Exhibition, Wilton House and grounds on an inclusive ticket – Adult: £5; Senior Citizens and Students: £4.50; Children over 5 years and under 16 years: £3.50.

Facilities: Free parking, an excellent self service restaurant and gift shop.

Disabled Access: Very suitable for disabled persons, ramps, lifts and disabled facilities.

Additional Information: No dogs are permitted except for guide dogs for the blind, we have a good picnic area.

WISLEY

Wisley, Woking, Surrey.
(0483) 224234

Status: The Royal Horticultural Society.

General Description: World-famous Royal Horticultural Society's garden showing every aspect of gardening within 250 acres of magnificent gardens. With wooded slopes planted with rhododendrons and azaleas, alpine meadows, rock gardens, herbaceous borders and pinetum there is something to enjoy in every season. There are specialist gardens, for example for disabled gardeners, small model gardens, flower and vegetable trials, glasshouse displays and an advisory service to help you with your own gardening problems.

Open: All year, Monday to Saturday (Sunday members only), 10 a.m. – 7 p.m.

Admission: Adult: £3.95; Children (6-16 years): £1.75, RHS members free. Disabled and visually handicapped visitors free.

Facilities: Licenced restaurant and self-service cafeteria.

Disabled Access: Disabled toilets. Wheelchair access. Free map of wheelchair route.

Additional Information: Guide dogs only. Picnic area near coach park. Advisory service.

WINKWORTH ARBORETUM

Hascombe Road, Godalming, GU8 4AD.
(048632) 477

Ownership: The National Trust.

Status: National Trust.

General Description: Hillside woodland with two lakes, many rare trees and shrubs. Peak displays, spring for bluebells and azaleas, autumn for colour, fine views.

Open: All year daily during daylight hours.

Admission: £2. No reduction for parties. Coach parties must book with Head Gardener tel. (048632) 477 to ensure parking space.

Facilities: Shop open 1st April to 15th November daily except Monday 2 a.m. – 6 p.m. or dusk if earlier. Saturday and Sunday only 11 a.m. – 6 p.m. Also open weekends in November to 22nd December and weekends in March. Open Bank Holiday Monday (closed Tuesday following). Christmas shop. Tearoom for light refreshments near upper car park, opening times as for shop but also open daily in May and October 11 a.m. – 6 p.m. for light lunches and teas. Booking with Concessionaire, Winkworth Arboretum near Godalming, Surrey (tel. Hascombe (048632) 265) when tearoom open).

Disabled Access: Limited access, viewpoint and lake from lower entrance are accessible.

Additional Information: Dogs must be kept on leads.

WOBURN ABBEY

Woburn, Bedfordshire, MK43 0TP.
(0525) 290666

Ownership: Marquess of Tavistock.

Status: Historic Houses Association.

General Description: Woburn Abbey houses a most impressive and important private collection of paintings, furniture, porcelain and silver by many of the world's great masters. The parkland surrounding the Abbey covers some 3,000 acres. Landscaped by Humphry Repton in the nineteenth century it contains nine species of deer, one of which is the Miles (often referred to as Pere David deer). There are extensive picnic areas, an antiques centre, pottery and camping extension. The private gardens and the maze will be open to visitors on the 27th April and 28th June 1992.

Open: 1st January to 28th March weekends only. 29th March to 1st November every day.

Admission: Park: £5 per car; Abbey – Adult: £5.50; Senior Citizens: £4; Children: £2. Deer Park admission charges do not apply to visitors purchasing their Abbey entrance ticket as they enter the park.

Facilities: Ample parking facilities for cars and coaches, self-service restaurant.

Disabled Access: Ambulant toilets, lift in house for wheelchairs but prior notice must be given.

Additional Information: Picnic areas, dogs allowed in park only on leashes.